WHAT I LEARNED HALF NAKED:

TALES OF A PRO CHEERLEADER

BY LESLIE SHAW HATCHARD

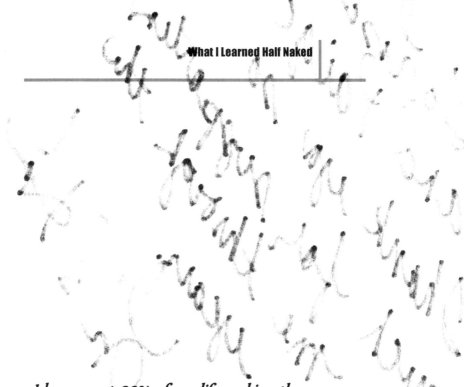

I have spent 90% of my life seeking the

approval and acceptance of others, this moment

is not one of them. I have opted to open this

door because I do not want to follow in

footsteps, I want to create them.

This book would have never come to fruition without the support, love, guidance and encouragement from so many wonderful and priceless people. I am forever grateful to each of you for helping me make my dream come true.

Special thanks to:

Mom and Dad, Scott, Kimberly Rhodes, Liz Collinsworth, Kim Harmon Gatlin, Cristen Benson, Rhetta Long, Melissa Sandlin, Brian Guilleaux, Lisa Holt, Joelene Walker, Bylee Jo Montomery, Kim Burge, Madison and Kennedy, Lance and Karen.

INTRODUCTION

Within these pages, I am going to expose some of the most difficult times I have experienced in my life. You will soon know my deepest fears and biggest failures. I am going to share with you the inside of a world that many people never imagined existed. Some of these experiences I have yet to share with my own family and several areas are still difficult for me to revisit. Before I can open this door, I need you to know something; I need you to

4

understand? Why I have chosen to write this book. This is not an easy question to answer because the reasons are so complex, therefore, I have no choice but to answer this question with a question. How could I not write this book? Everyone has a story, and they have a right to tell it. This is my life, and I feel my story needs to be heard.

It is my belief that everything that you do or fail to do has power, be it negative or positive. It has taken me over ten years to write this book because I don't like to hurt people. It has never been my intention to bad mouth or even discourage anyone from entering into the professional cheerleading industry, however, many people for one reason

or another are going to be upset over the

content of this book. The reason for this is of

no concern to me anymore. When someone is

angry because you told the truth, it is a

negative force in your life. I have chosen to

openly share my life with others in an effort to

create positive changes in the industry.

I am telling my story to allow others to

see the peace it brings me to know that God

thought so much of me that he didn't give up.

As I continue to grow and move on in my life, I

feel compelled and obligated to share what I

have learned with others. Regardless of what

issues are at hand, the lessons we learn in life

are generally all the same. With all the differences we care to see in each other, we share a common desire: the need to feel we were created on purpose...by God.

My story is just that, my story. I don't claim to speak for anyone else but myself. Some things within and between the text of this book are unpleasant, but in order to help you understand how I lost and discovered myself again, I must reveal all I can bring myself to write. I do so without any intention of causing harm or placing fault on anyone, as we are all learning. I was a willing participant in the path that I chose and make no excuses for my own naïve and sometimes careless judgments.

Instead, I am here to celebrate and salute my journey that has brought me to a place in life many people don't find. In my professional cheerleading career, I met so many wonderful people that if I hadn't discovered myself, I can honestly say that it would have all been worth it anyway.

1
Hoodwinked by Choice

I am often perplexed by the nasty things people are capable of doing to one another. I am even more nauseated by the evil things people so willingly do to themselves. I have learned that people would rather give their God given power to another person before taking the slightest chance to believe in themselves. By allowing an outsider to set the standard and tone for which they live their lives. As soon as we are born, the world (society) begins to shift us in and out of levels, places us in boxes and sizes us up. All with our permission of course. For some reason, we seem to be able to process the various individuals better when we can size them up and break them down into categories. This wouldn't be problem if "the boxing of people" was not accompanied with so many judgments, assumptions and expectations. Let me be clear; when I say judgments I am not referring to basic right and wrong, or anything to do with the law, I am speaking of unwritten social rules that have no real basis or significance. Somebody, somewhere, a long time ago decided that A+B=C and we just go with it without question or challenge. Here are a few examples to get your mind turning:

"If you're of one race, you should marry within that race."

"Rich is good, poor is bad."

"If you're short and fat, you are unattractive"

"If you have ovaries you shouldn't play football."

Unfortunately, we cannot always control the way society chooses to perceive each of us. We can, however, control how you see ourselves.

People don't have to buy into the society's idea of success, beauty or anything else. In America, at least, each person can decide for his or her self if the worlds' opinions are right or they can look within themselves, and then form their own definitions. Each of us has the opportunity to decide who we are, what job we want, where we want to live, who we vote for, or what food we want to eat. We have the power to choose to be Baptist, Catholic, Muslim or none of the above. One of my favorites is that if you don't like the name your parents bestowed upon you, you can change it! It's great to have choices. However, more often than not, people, including myself, do not honor our own power, and side with society. In doing so, we create mental crutches that keep us from being who God created us to be, and we can't seem to find the courage to be the person we can be.

To me, a crutch is a goal that we set that is directly connected to the success of all other aspirations. It is the one thing you want so badly that your life won't be complete until you obtain it.   In the meantime, life and happiness are on hold until the goal is achieved. A crutch can include anything you hide behind or lean upon. A crutch can involve living in a certain neighborhood or always needing to hear that you are attractive. A crutch can even be something good like maintaining a certain grade point average. When it comes to our physical appearances, we often see negative crutches. We often find ourselves wanting a smaller nose, fuller lips, bigger breasts or to wear a smaller dress size. More commonly, crutches can be landing that promotion, being accepted into a specific social group or maybe being the perfect mother. A crutch is anything that is used as an excuse and keeps one from complete happiness and self-acceptance. Some crutches are inherited for example, ethnic background and being born into social class, but I believe we give ourselves the most viscous and self-destructive crutches. I is a dangerous thing to look outside of ourselves for fulfillment, validation, approval or value.

Like most people, I have depended upon several crutches, but the one crutch that almost destroyed me was the "cheerleader crutch." If you don't know what it is like to depend upon, don't fret, just replace the word "cheerleader" with "business owner", "married", "out-of-debt", "famous", or maybe "lotto winner". Pick your very own personal poison

Somewhere along the way, my ego decided that possessing the title of "professional cheerleader" held everything I did not: fame, poise, beauty, confidence, sexuality, talent and glamour. All of the things, of course, I deeply desired. I convinced myself that I would have to become this phenomenon called a "cheerleader" to prove my own worth to not only myself, but the world. So began my journey.

As you probably have already figured out, when I meet my goal of becoming a cheerleader the result was not what I expected. I did not get to put away my crutch because none of the things I had been looking to collect were there. So, instead of turning around and running out the door, I just hung around… for the next 13 years. For more than a decade, I depended upon my crutch. I searched and searched, believed in everything but my own significance, let myself be led and allowed myself to be lost. It is my own fault that I fell into this pattern in my life.

2

WHO WAS SHE?

My greatest disappointment in life would be to leave the world exactly the way I found it. At the end of each day, when the house is quiet, I like to take time to reflect. I think about what I did and who I talked with. I think about the situations I found myself in, and my reactions to them. What did I do and could I have done some things differently? Did I encourage and exercise patience? Did I handle challenging situations in a way that I was proud of? It has always been a priority for me to continue to grow and learn from my mistakes.   The most important question I ask myself is, how short did I fall from being the person I want to be? Am I a person who embodies character, integrity love, compassion and individuality or am I lost and caught up in the world?

Today I spent most of the morning taking care of my infant daughter, paying some bills and folding laundry. Later in the afternoon, I began to do some cleaning and before I know it, my husband Scott, is home from work. Soon after he arrived it was time for me to head out to my job. This particular day I taught five dance classes and returned home around 9:45 p.m. and when I walked in,

Scott and the baby were playing before

bedtime. After Scott and Madison were sound

asleep I was able to settle down for a hot bath

and a much deserved glass of wine. I

reviewed the day's activities and made a list of

things that needed to be done:

1. Call Renee

2. Scrub walkway entrance

3. Choreograph

4. Make Doctor appointment

5. Buy diapers

When the to do list was complete, I noticed a

detail that I hadn't really paid much attention to

before: I could not think of one thing that I ate

today. Come to think of it, I couldn't even remember what I had to eat yesterday or the day before. The reason I could not recall is because I had eaten very little to nothing at all. Without a doubt this isn't normal, and that was clear to me, but what wasn't clear was why? So for the first time in a long time, I asked myself, "why am I doing this?" And I listened…

The more I opened up and looked at myself from the other side, the more I did not like what I saw. I was not at all the person I thought I was. Instead of the courageous and confident woman I was pretending to believe I was, I found almost every part of my life was influenced by things other than me. Who was this woman and, more importantly, when did I become her and stop believing in myself and my own importance? The real me was hiding beneath layers of unacknowledged disappointment, self hatred, sadness and confusion.   I knew in that moment that I needed to find a way to pull back all the layers to find myself again. I did not want my daughter to call this person "Mom".

In my thoughts that followed, I found that the area of emptiness in my life consistently led me back to the same source. Although my ten years in the professional cheerleading industry were over, I still lived each day, as if I was half naked wearing a

21

uniform. I would soon find out that this dysfunction was not without reason; I was still seen as an American phenomenon, a cheerleader. When I began my career, I believed I was aiming to become the epitome of a woman. I wanted to be respected, talented, attractive, intelligent, empowered and a role model. I had no idea that this career would leave me far from all of attributes I imagined. I discovered that I wanted to be skinny more than anything and found myself valuing the constant approval of others in every aspect of my life. I allowed myself to fall short of, what I thought was, the ideal woman and bought into the opinions of others and, as a result, cheated myself out of the chance to be the person God intended.

Whenever people would inquire about my cheerleading experience, I wouldn't hesitate to respond in an extremely positive way, no matter what the question, as if my mind wasn't my own. While replying, with a smile on my face, a part of my brain would continuously give me a completely different response. I supported the belief that cheerleading was a glamorous and rewarding career path, in every way, and constantly told myself to thank my lucky stars that I was chosen to be allowed to have this amazing experience. I loyally contributed to the illusion that I was completely validated as a beautiful and powerful woman with my membership to this exclusive society. Instead of saying what I knew to be my true experience, and before I could find the courage to say what I really believed, the voice I recognized to be my own lied as it had been trained to do.

Always looking to find the good, I forgot how small and unimportant I felt as a cheerleader. At a time when I should have been filled with confidence, I was struggling to be less of who I was and more of who they wanted me to be: the shell of a person aiming to be less of everything I am. I learned how to be less black, less fat, less smart, less human, less compassionate, and less real in order to be more appealing. My self-esteem was compromised while I was buying into the belief that making myself look and act like a doll would be rewarding. I deeply believed that someone else's version of perfect hair, nails, make-up and helping me say just the right words would bring me success and happiness.

"Saturday Night Live" used to have a skit that was called "perfect cheer" by Craig and Arianna on. I was the "perfect cheerleader". For over ten years I played the role for the Dallas Cowboys, the Dallas Mavs and The Dallas Burn. I thought these experiences would make me a stronger person by boosting my confidence and teaching me how to be a more successful, contributing member of society. Starting out so young, I was influenced more than I can ever express

25

and in more ways than I will ever realize. My biggest problem was that I was left without the formula to transition out of the cheerleader role. Painfully and beautifully, while on life's journey looking to find myself again, I also found the meaning of life. I was created and sent here in perfect condition to fulfill my own destiny. I was not sent here to learn what I needed to be myself; God already took care of that. The environment we live in nurtures powerless people, and would falsely have us believe that we are better off when we obtain power and strength from outside of ourselves.

,

3
SMOKE AND MIRRORS

Surprisingly and ironically, the myths that surround professional cheerleading have been brilliantly created. They want us to see an image of what they have decided is perfect woman. She is presented as the total package of wealth, class, glamour and beauty.

However, this image is slightly twisted. I don't mean to imply that the "All-American" sport of cheerleading is all awful. I have many fantastic memories of friendship, laughter and experiences to look back on. I am most thankful to have had the opportunity to do what

I love, to perform dance. I'll just let you read on and judge for yourself.

The biggest of many misconceptions is that cheerleaders live a particular lifestyle. For whatever reason, people imagine that cheerleaders earn large sums of money and live a life of glamour and ease. When the truth, in reality, is that we couldn't live on the salary alone. We would be fortunate to keep our gas tank full with the money made in this industry. Regardless, most professional cheerleading organizations require that you either work full-time or be a full-time student.

My cheerleading salary ranged between

$20.00 and $50.00 per game, but it is

not unusual for dancers to earn up to

$100.00 per game as salaries vary by

city. At first, this may seem to be a

decent amount of income, and while

there are a small number of professional

cheerleaders that are paid for rehearsal

time, no team in Texas has ever been

compensated for rehearsal time.

Considering the significant role

cheerleader's play in the overall success

of a sports organization and the

astronomical amount athletes (who

deserve every penny) are paid; it is just

a drop in the bucket. Keep in mind that

there are NO endorsement deals for

individual cheerleaders. They can be

cast in a commercial, star in a reality

show and NEVER receive a dime.

Printed materials, like calendars, mugs,

tee shirts, books and posters, are sold in

abundance without any compensation

going to the cheerleaders.   Taking into

account the countless hours and

dedication that is necessary to be

successful, compensation is low!

The public is only exposed to what is

presented to them on the court or field, so they

do not know the amount of time required

behind the scenes. The rehearsal schedule to

prepare for each game can be grueling. I still remember practicing one to five times per week and meeting two to four hours before games to rehearse. Think about this in terms of hours a week...four to 20 hours a week given to an organization for free that generates millions upon millions of dollars per year. I'm not really sure what the reasoning stands behind such low pay, other than the fact that no one has ever complained loud enough. I think the organizations pay dancers/cheerleaders poorly simply because they can! I don't know about other teams, but the

Dallas Mavericks would simply say, "It is not in the budget". Is that really an answer or an excuse? That budget must be pretty small because everything else the dancers receive besides pay comes from sponsorship. Sponsors play a bigger role in supporting the dancers than the employer by supplying shoes, tights, warm-ups, bags, several costumes, etc. Perhaps the budget is so small because the organization doesn't acknowledge the level of difficulty or respect the job. They think that those girls are just shaking their butts and should feel privileged for the opportunity to do it on their time and court.

The Dallas Cowboys Cheerleaders boldly give excuses for such an insignificant salary by claiming that, "they don't want girls to just cheer for the money" and "it is tradition."

My only problem with this is that there is an

elite group within the Dallas Cowboys

Cheerleaders called the "Show Group." The

Show Group consists of roughly 12 girls

chosen to go on USO tours all over the world

entertaining troops and performing at other

appearances. This group of dancers is paid.

So, I'm a little confused about the sincerity

behind their reasoning. I also have a problem

not paying cheerleaders well because the

organizations make an astronomical amount of

money off the cheerleaders, their appearances

and paraphernalia. The least they could do is

make sure they compensate the cheerleaders

accordingly.

During my years as Assistant Director of the Dallas Mavericks Dancers I was bothered when I discovered that these organizations believe that these girls were their property. They wanted the girl's time, expecting them to be available at the drop of a hat for appearances without compensation. I personally know this to be true because I was in charge of arranging dancers for events and appearances. Special appearances, of course, are a vital part of being a cheerleader/dancer. It is also of utmost importance as a tool between sports organization and their clients. I personally found them to be a rewarding part of my career and did a large number of them. As the Assistant Director I had a contract

approved that required three weeks' notice for

a request consideration, it was a common

occurrence for the organization to contact me

within days of an event requesting

cheerleaders. Three weeks seemed to be

ample time for the dancers to check their

individual class schedules, rearrange

appointments, request off from jobs or other

commitments. After all, these women aren't

sitting at home, waiting by the phone. They

have lives, jobs, families and responsibilities.

Although the Mavs' requests were often not

within the rules of the agreement, I would try to

make it happen anyway. Sometimes it worked

out for everyone involved, but other time is

wasn't so easy. When it didn't work out, I was

responsible for letting the organization know

that the dancers would not be available for that

particular event. End of the story, right?

Wrong! It was only the beginning. As

expected, the person I had originally been

working with reported back to their superior

that the girls were unable to commit, and more

drama began after the superior re-called me to

ask again if the dancers were available. Of

course, I repeated the process of checking with

the girls to see if anything had possibly

changed. If things were different then great, if

not, the panic continued. The superior would

then tattle to my boss that I couldn't get any

dancers to appear, and complain that they

were desperate for dancers. If they were that in

need of dancers, they should have planned

36

ahead and followed the rules. The truth is that

the dancers are so low on the totem pole that

people used them as pawns and committed

them to events without any prior arrangements.

There is nothing better than catching an

advertisement on TV, radio or in print

announcing that you will be appearing

somewhere, before even knowing about it. All

I wish is that they treated the very low

maintenance dancers with ¼ of the respect

they treat the higher maintenance players.

Probably the biggest shocker to people

is that it is very rare for a dancer or

cheerleader to date player. The Dallas

Cowboys Cheerleaders, along with most

organizations' policies regarding fraternizing

with players is clear. Cheerleaders are told

repeatedly that they are NOT to date the

players. In fact, they are NOT to date anyone

in the organization! I have never dated or

known anyone who has cheered for a team

and then dated one of the players. Ironically,

cheerleaders don't have a lot of close contact

with the men they root on, besides the rare

personal appearance they may have together,

on the sidelines, or passing in the hall. In

addition to this obstacle, many organizations

have strict rules forbidding the dating of

players. Violating this rule gets you promptly

kicked off of the team. During my season with

the Cowboys a young lady was kicked off the

team for breaking this rule. I have only seen

38

this policy broken and enforced once in 16 years. That doesn't mean it doesn't happen more frequently, it just means that neither me nor my friends were involved. I would be kidding myself to think that some girls didn't cheer just hoping to have the opportunity to get closer to the players. That is definitely a hell of a lot of work to meet a man! I don't necessarily have an issue with the policy, my only reservation is in wondering, are the players told that they are NOT allowed to date the cheerleaders?....NOT

Next time you go to a game, I hope that you will look past the cloud of glamour, glitz and bull#@*^ to see the extraordinary women who are mothers, wives, teachers, students

and daughters busting their rears while making

it look effortless to entertain you.

4

LIVING DOLLS

I am repeatedly intrigued by how people react when they find out that I was a professional cheerleader. People of all ages and all walks of life automatically feel as though they are in the presence of something good, special and right upon meeting me. If I've met them through some type of dance venue they are even more impressed. After all, cheerleading is a big deal in Texas and can be as addicting as Friday night football. From pee wee, to Jr. High, to high school and

41

college, cheerleading shapes the wholesome

image of the All-American girl. Anyone who

has ever been a cheerleader or wanted to be

one recognizes how validating becoming a

cheerleader can be. Whether we agree or not,

holding that title will open doors and carry

power throughout a lifetime.

We all remember the *Texas*

Cheerleader Story, don't we? The mother of

one cheerleading candidate wanted so badly

for her daughter to be on the cheerleading

squad that she hired a hit man to kill the rival's

mother. Cheerleading, on any level, is an

extracurricular activity that triggers something

in people. That mom wanted her daughter to

feel the validation she thought cheerleading would give her, and let's be honest the Mom was probably looking for a little validation for herself. She wanted her daughter to feel pretty, accepted and special.

Webster defines a doll to be a "child's toy made to resemble a human being, any attractive or lovable person, to dress stylishly or showily." Professional cheerleading does a perfect job of creating and reinforcing an image of women that I can define in no other way but as a living doll. As I picture the small girl I was not so long ago, I wonder why playing contently with my baby doll brought me so much happiness. What was it about that doll that held my attention?   It seems so obvious;

she was pretty and perfect in every way, from

her neatly polished toe nails to her thinly

painted lips. Her hair always smelled the way

it did the first day I got her and she never said

a word. This doll gave me unconditional

entertainment and love until I had no need for

her. Whatever I wished her to be, she

became.

How could you possibly turn a living,

thinking woman into a living doll? It is really

pretty simple: Dress her up, change and fix her

hair, and tell her what and what not to say. On

her way out the door, whisper in her ear that

she is too fat, not pretty or smart, that she will

probably fall on her face, and that it was an accident that she is on the team. Now go out there and do a great job!

To establish control, you must go through the breakdown and build up process. This is what the Dallas Cowboys Cheerleaders do so well and is one reason why they are so incredibly successful in the cheerleading industry. After making the squad, the first meeting is spent in a room designated for Cowboys press conferences. The first thing you hear is "YOU ARE NOT A DALLAS COWBOYS CHEERLEADER, AND YOU WON'T BE UNTIL THE END OF THE SEASON WHEN YOU GET YOUR PINKIE

45

RING." After this, you cover an endless list of rules you must follow. I believe that rules are good, in fact I would go so far as to say that I love rules and structure. The DCC have many of what I consider to be "normal" rules, such as arriving at the games a certain number of hours before kickoff, how to take care of your uniform, no fraternizing with players, etc. Rules should be set to keep order, not to control people. It is similar to the difference between a church and a cult, in expectations. I'm not saying that cheerleading is a cult, but you can't ignore its cult-like tendencies. Review some of the rules and judge for yourself:

1. Make-up must be worn everywhere outside of your house (no matter what, even to the corner store).

2. You must answer "Yes, ma'am. Thank you" when spoken to by the directors and veteran cheerleaders, no matter what rude or derogatory thing they may say.

3. Veteran cheerleaders are always right.

4. Do not have your picture professionally made in your uniform.

5. If you are a model, you must stop modeling.

6. Color nail polish must be worn at all times.

I could truly go on for days with the extreme

things they want you to do.   These rules

seemed so silly and unnecessary! The rookies

are routinely treated without respect and are

degraded on a regular basis by veteran

cheerleaders and the administration. After the

endless list of guidelines, from pearl earrings to

nail polish at all times, is gone over and

understood, we move on to the "you're not

good enough to be here" stage of the meeting.

The administration goes down a list of things

that they hate about you while everyone else is

listening. Examples include, "Sandy, don't

ever, ever pull your hair behind your ears, they

stick out too much," or "Tina, that blue eye

shadow is so small town," and "Jamie, your

upper arms are too fat." Out of about 40

48

comments, maybe 3 are positive. During my year, the girl who received the comment about her ears never came to another practice...she just wasn't there anymore. Back then, I couldn't believe she would give up such an opportunity but now, I understand. She was simply making a choice.

Rehearsals took place Monday-Thursday (sometimes Friday) from 6:45 p.m. until 10:30 p.m. During this time, we rehearsed routine after routine, and rehearsed, and rehearsed. If you've ever seen a Dallas Cowboys Cheerleader routine, you would understand that the choreography is not difficult at all. Practices last so long because

49

they choose girls based on looks rather than talent (rehearsals should last two hours at the most) but understandably, everyone stays until it looks good. Some practices were held outside on the Cowboys practice

field and at Texas Stadium. At no time during practice were you ever permitted to drink water. This was supposedly done to prepare your body for vigorous, hot and long game days. I never really quite understood this, considering that the cheerleaders <u>are</u> allowed water on game day. Maybe it's because all of America is watching.

I've suffered from asthma from a very young age and use an inhaler daily and I remember trying to hide my asthma so the director wouldn't have a reason to kick me off. It was very stressful on game days. I would secretly attach my inhaler to the inside of my boot just in case I needed it on the field. When it was my turn to get a drink I would move close to the stadium wall and remove my inhaler to get a puff. I would also take a double dose of ephenephrine pills to ensure that I would make it through the game.

I distinctly remember always being watched and feeling as though I didn't belong and that I was always being sized up. As far as weight was concerned, lists were posted in the locker room door listing the cheerleaders' names and a comment about their figure. Mine

always said hips and thighs. Some others said

knees, upper arms, waist, etc. This list was

posted on the locker room door for every

person who passed by to see. Why not just

put it in your individual locker? Apparently, you

gain more control of someone by degrading

her among her teammates.

A friend that I met in college with was

also a rookie cheerleader, and we confessed to

each other that we wished we would have had

a wreck on our way to rehearsal so we didn't

have to go. That is truly how bad it felt being

there. I was surrounded by hungry, angry,

psychotic Barbies. We never knew what was

going to come at us. It felt like we were

mentally training for a war. All of this was not

necessary for a football game and if it was,

some changes need to be made.

At this point, I felt worthless and

overwhelmed with all the rules while wondering

how in the world I got to this place. However,

next comes what at first appears to be a small

light at the end of the tunnel, a makeover

including: make-up, fake hair, and fake nails.

Most everything about you is changed and

altered to help you look and act like a

cheerleader. I am assuming that the

administration has a list in its head of what a

Dallas Cowboys Cheerleader should look like.

At first glance, it all seems so nice. You feel pretty and glamorous and, of course, you would never object to any changes even if deep down you hated them. If you do object, you run the risk of appearing as though being a cheerleader is not the most important thing in your life. You want to be on the team, don't you? Well, they know you do. When the administration says you don't have to do anything you don't feel comfortable with, you agree to their demands anyway, like all the others. Bleach, trim, dye, lose weight... you do it all. You already know that refusing to conform to their standards and rules could be taken as a lack of dedication potentially leading

54

to you being called into the office and greeted
with a lovely invitation to leave.

After a while, you get so used to
changing things about yourself that you don't
even consider your true feelings any longer.
After watching girls go before you and make
mistakes, you eventually get to a place where
you will do anything to make them
(management) like you. I will never forget the
first day back from Christmas break. Things
were mostly the same except that along with
looking well-rested, some girls looked a little
different physically. Some had gained weight
in their chests, some had lost weight in other
areas and a few noses looked a little slimmer.

I was so naive and it took me a day or two to realize that over the holiday, some girls took a little excursion to the plastic surgeon. Of course, the administration never encouraged permanent physical alterations (it's not what you say, it's what you do) but you can bet the ranch that those who took it upon themselves to make some physical alterations, were being featured on the next poster and calendar. The game was so easy to follow...if you were willing to play. I live for the day that a male athlete's talent and success is hinged on the size of his manhood.

When changing your physical appearance becomes so customary and second nature, so does altering your mental

appearance. One of the rules we had was that

you couldn't do any interviews without going

through the organization. No photos could be

taken of you outside of the organization (even

if you're a model). Control. You see, they don't

want you to be a real person with your own

thoughts and opinions. They want you to be a

cut out of an image, the cookie cutter

cheerleader. They have to control what

everyone on the outside hears and sees. I

don't really understand what they're afraid of.

When you put on that uniform, make no

mistake about it, you aren't yourself anymore.

You are a possession, a piece of

property…you are owned. They truly want

people to see the doll and the company that

manufactured her, if it weren't illegal, I wouldn't put it past them to brand their cheerleaders. Who you are and what you think was and is irrelevant. I say this because when you change any part of yourself to please another, it will affect you in the most hidden parts of your soul. Make sure you believe in the institution but first make sure the institution believes in you.

5
INVISIBLE BARRIERS

Watching my husband, Scott, and my daughter, Madison, discover each other brings me a lifetime of joy and gratitude. He patiently watches her try some new skill, like standing on her own, never turning away for long so that when she falls, he can save her from learning how hard the floor is. The relief in his eyes and

59

the wonder of his strength in her eyes parallels my feelings for my father now, but especially when I was growing up and discovering the world and its truths.

Any father would go to lengths to warn his baby girl of how cold the world can be or at least cushion the fall. The falls that my father fears for me most are the ones that come without warning or logic and can leave deep, ugly scars.

The day I will never forget is the day I was hanging out in Tracy Widding's room, a fellow Showstopper (our school dance team), while attending Navarro Junior College in Corsicana, Texas. As we were getting to know each other, she pulled out a squad photo of the world famous Dallas Cowboy's Cheerleaders (Tracy was going to try out for the squad soon). I, of course, was excited for her but I was not one of those little girls who had always wanted to grow up and become a cheerleader. I just wanted to grow up and be a dancer like my big sister, Karen. I had never thought about auditioning for DCC until Tracy invited me to come with her to the audition. Not knowing that the rest of my life would be shaped by my decision I said, "Sure".

While waiting for the audition day to arrive, excitement and fear were building. I began to hear stories of how hard it was to make the team. It is not uncommon for girls to audition six or even seven times before making it and I was still not fully prepared for the number of girls who were planning to audition just like we were.

The audition day came and something happened that I couldn't have seen coming. Tracy and I arrived at Texas Stadium early, but not nearly early enough. When we arrived, the registration line was as least 100 girls long. My first thought was that I had no idea this sort of thing was such a big deal to so many people.

My second thought was, how do I get out of this? We patiently waited in line, finally got to the registration table, got our audition number and warmed up to dance. After all, I was there to dance, so let's get it over with, I thought.

As the audition process began, the organization's leaders explained how things would run. We listened closely and followed each request to the letter. Six girls were to line up in front of the judges' table. One by one you were to announce your name, age, occupation, and why you were auditioning. After each girl had spoken, the entire group was to step away from the judges table into a staggered line. The gentleman in charge of music then plays a random top forty music selection for about one and a half to two minutes. During this time, which seems like an eternity, you are supposed to dance...freestyle (anything goes). When the music finally stops you stop dancing, switch lines and repeat. This process is continued all day until each candidate had gone before the panel of judges. After the last group has left the floor, and no call backs are requested, every auditionee is dismissed. Prior to leaving the stadium, a time is announced for you to return to see who made it to the next round of competition.

Tracy and I had a great time talking and watching the other girls. I considered the experience fun and did not regret doing it. But I also did not believe I would ever be chosen. As we returned to find out the results, I must admit I had become very nervous and so had Tracy. When we drove up we could already see a crowd out front of the stadium checking the numbers that were posted on the window of the entrance. If you saw your number, it meant you had been chosen and were going on to the next round. As Tracy and I impatiently approached the list, I don't think either of us were breathing. We saw ahead of us some girls react in tears of devastation and others with screams of delight, and a few just quietly walked away. To my joy and sadness I looked at the list and saw that my number was posted but Tracy's was not. Unbelievable! As she congratulated me and I consoled her, I tried to let the reality set in. I also quickly reminded myself that this was just the first step in a long process. I would have to return the following week and start auditioning all over again.

Still in disbelief, I returned early the next Saturday to give it another go. By this point I was really getting in to the challenge, and became very excited and nervous. I also kept reminding myself that I still had one more step to go in order to make it to finals. Registration was early and we had to get new numbers before the competition could begin. After check-in, the choreographer teaches a jazz and kick routine, which I still remember today. The choreographer teaches each group of six dancers the routines and, as you can imagine, this takes a long time. After all the groups have gone, there is a short break and then the girls get to show their stuff to the judges. Each group performs their routines and does both right and left leg splits. Then you play the long and painful waiting game.

The day started at 8 a.m. and the judges did not return with the results until about 5 p.m. Thank God that this time the contestants didn't have to leave the stadium while the judges cast their votes. As the judges re-enter the area, tension and excitement overcame the room, and butterflies filled my stomach. I was almost certain that my number would not be called. When they are about to announce who advances they always play that stupid song, "If My Friends Could See Me Now". The only reason I think the song is so stupid is because every time I hear it, to this day, I get anxious and start to sweat. Waiting for them to announce your number is pure torture, especially if you are at the end of the list. Well I was lucky, and I use that word with caution, once again. I had made it to the finals. I felt like I had won the lotto, minus the fact that I didn't get any money.

After all the finalists are called out, each girl gets an information packet which holds all the requirements for the final audition, to be held two weeks from that day. After reading through the material, you would think I was applying to go to college except for the fact that you have to do LESS to be accepted into a university. Don't get me wrong, I was happy to do all of it at the time. Looking back, I fail to understand if it mattered at all or if it's to see exactly how many hoops you are willing to jump through.

First, I had a personal interview with the Director. I can't remember anything that we discussed. I had to write a composition based on a list of questions, as well as prepare for a test over Cowboys trivia. The test consisted of questions like "Who makes the Cheerleaders Uniforms?", "Who won the Heisman Trophy?", "Who is in the ring of Honor?", "Draw the offensive and defensive line up", etc. Let's not forget that all while preparing for this, you had to be ready on audition day to show a two minute "talent" routine.

Okay, let's talk about my talent. I did a dance routine and I can say with complete honesty, what the hell was I thinking? I did some goofy, deep and serious modern dance filled with meaning and emotion because at the time that is what I was studying in college. I guess I was buying into the notion that they wanted to see what was on the inside of me. After I

watched some other routines, I saw that it was definitely not the forum to show my dance piece, but to shake my piece of......whatever.

Nonetheless, the carpet ride that I was on had run out of magic. During the last round of auditions, the song came on. You know the song, "If My Friends could See Me Now". I was still glued to my seat at the end of the announcement of the finalist. My number was not called to come up and join the other training camp candidates. Disappointed and low, I gathered my bags to meet my father who was waiting outside to take me home.

Even though I was feeling very low, just leave it to me to find the light at the end of the tunnel. As I was walking toward the exit, the Assistant Director stopped me and said with a big grin, "lose a little weight and come back next year". I was like..."Cool...will do!" That was that, until I went to the car and told my Dad what had happened. After the long walk to the car, naturally my father wanted to know what I hoped he wouldn't. He wanted to know how things went and softly I replied to him that I did not make the squad. There was a short pause before he responded by asking, "Why?" After sharing the audition results and what I had been told by the Assistant Director, I saw a

72

side of my father that I had never seen before. He became angry and looked as if his blood was starting to boil. I didn't really understand why he reacted in this way until later. Although I was trying to remain cool about my reaction in front of my father, seeing him respond in such a way hit me harder than not making it. I put my head down and cried all the way home. I was crying because I didn't make the team, but I was also crying because I thought that I had unknowingly caused pain to my father who I adored. During the ride home, I worried how the rest of my family would react. I wished that I could somehow get out of telling them, but I choked it out quickly and went straight to bed. After a few hours of therapeutic sleep, I woke up to a room filled with red roses from my family.

After a few weeks had passed and the melodrama of not making the team had worn off, I started to think about my upcoming travel overseas to dance. One Sunday, I attended church with my family, but I arrived separately and at a later time and had to sit in the balcony away from them. As the service was coming to an end, I heard a voice through the microphone that sounded familiar to me; it was my father's voice.

The sermon that Sunday was about the times in your life when you find yourself up against a wall, a wall that you can't get over without a strong and deep faith in a higher power. Sometimes in life you just have to walk in the pair of shoes that God gave you and do the best you can. What the shoes look like is irrelevant, so is how much they weigh. Just be sure you walk in <u>those</u> shoes and don't make the mistake of walking in the dark.

Although I could not see him yet, I accepted that the voice I heard was my Daddy's. I heard very clearly in his voice that he was upset. While Pastor Wesley comforted him, he shared with our church family every detail of the experience that I had just lived through with the cheerleader auditions. I had no idea that my ordeal had touched him enough to cry. I was heartbroken all over again. How painful for a father to have to witness his own flesh and blood learn that there really are no "happily ever afters". The sermon touched and moved my Father so deeply because I had seen my first invisible barrier. I would soon learn that was not my last and I would not truly comprehend this theory for another year.

After the tryouts were over, what do you think I did for an entire year? All I did was think about and prepare to go back and audition again. Remember, my parents taught me well. If you want something bad enough, it's worth fighting for. I was not going to give up by not auditioning again. In the blink of an eye, the Dallas Cowboy's Cheerleader tryouts were here and I was ready. I lost a total of five pounds!! Ha, that'll show 'em. I honestly was a little worried about this, but my fears were hushed when at the preliminaries a former cheerleader, who was helping run tryouts, said she could tell I had lost some weight. She thought I looked awesome and that was proof enough for me. What a spiral of crap!

Anyway, I made it through the first two rounds of auditions and during the finals I was riding on that magic carpet again. My number was called to be a training camp candidate and I then went on to be one of America's sweethearts, a Dallas Cowboys Cheerleader. This year went by twice as fast as the previous, and I soon had to decide if I should re-audition for the squad again. I was really nervous about this because I knew that the outcome could go either way. Realizing this was a possibility, I humbly reflected on the past year. I always knew the choreography, I was religiously prompt, I performed 110%, I never opened my mouth, I smiled constantly, I was thin, etc. but I still felt uneasy. In retrospect, this was my intuition that I had not yet learned to follow. I think I went through with the audition anyway because of the meeting I had with the Director. At the end of the season, the Director meets with each cheerleader to discuss any problems. She said there were none with me.

Well, just wake yourself up and smell the cappuccino! The third time I would hear that special song ("If My Friends Could See Me Know") would not be the charm. My number was never called and, as you can imagine, I was devastated, for the lack of a better word. Buckets of tears flowed but, after a few hours, I was okay. I predictably remembered that if you want something, you work for it even if the work is hard. So, I made a plan. Don't forget the light at the end of the tunnel! If it is there I will find it.

In my strange way of thinking I was convinced that I must have gotten fat, pissed somebody off or just sucked during my performance at auditions. You have to understand that I was not any longer upset about not making it. I just wanted to dance, and I was willing to work and pay my dues to get that. If I screwed up, I'd do better next time. Hopelessly hopeful, sometimes I made myself sick with this. Somebody needs to hurry up and write a song about it.

Anyway, my next step was to call the Cowboys Cheerleader headquarters, as suggested by the choreographer, and set up an appointment with the Director. I was grateful that she met with me because I know she didn't have to. Unfortunately, I left more confused than before I went

She started the meeting by saying that she had nothing negative to say. She stated good qualities about me like I had lots of fans, I was thin, my "look" was good. But then she said something that took me by surprise. **She had to "pick a certain amount of girls that were just pretty".** If she didn't think that wasn't negative, I don't know what is.

81

You probably can imagine how that made me feel all warm and fuzzy inside. I politely thanked her for meeting with me and left the office. I sat in the car and let what she had said to me sink in. After about ten minutes I asked myself, "how do I fix that?" Where do I start? How could I begin to compete against that? In that instant I got it...INVISIBLE BARRIERS...I get it. I didn't want to look for the light any longer, I just wanted to get out of the tunnel as fast a I could. I decided that I was beat! I never re-auditioned again.

6

ISSUES

I consider myself fortunate and blessed to have a group of real sister-friends. The kind of good friends that you are spiritually connected to. Girlfriends that know what you're thinking before you have a chance to say it. Always able to see how badly you're hurting inside, even if you try to hide it. Lisa and Kimberly (both former professional cheerleaders), those are my girls! I'm sure that in our heads we think we click so well because we love to laugh, like the same things or simply because we are all former cheerleaders. "Issues" are the glue that bonds us together.

Lisa and Kimberly know exactly what I am referring to. "Issues" is one of those words that good friends have. It needs no explanation or excuse; it just is and will always mean the same thing for the rest of our lives. It affectionately refers to the self-hatred of physical image and the need to continuously measure up to a standard that no one can even define. Each of us have arrived at this common place at different times, but with tragically similar circumstances.

Looking back, I understand and regret that when you live a crazy life, you inevitably make crazy choices. When you can't control anything, the one thing you can control turns you inside out. In the blink of an eye, I found myself in a place where I thought I would never be...a sad place, where someone's opinion of your body blacks out everything else. It slowly conceals reality and consumes your entire life.

85

As a professional cheerleader, appearance (more specifically weight), is understandably a major part of being successful in the industry. On the other hand, so is being a talented dancer, but these two attributes don't always complement one another. The successful dancer/cheerleader is commonly talented because of the many hours of physically hard work, sweat and mental dedication to the art form. Ironically, as a result of this, she is then left with a beautiful "dancer's body;" muscular legs, a strong rear, and hardly ever having a large chest.

Eating disorders are ramped in the cheerleading industry. We can never find out how bad it really is because it's not talked about, not even among friends. In fact, Lisa, Kimberly and I only discussed it after our careers were over. It reminds me of President Clinton's quote, don't ask don't tell. *Don't ask* because it's too painful and *don't tell* because deep down you want what they have, thinness.

When I cheered with Lisa and she was not eating regularly, before I found myself caught in this web of nothingness, I actually admired her. As expected, I encouraged her to eat, if you can call asking once encouraging. I'm ashamed of that now. In my head, I thought she was too thin and I could actually see all of her ribs. I found myself longing to look just like her. I remember in Mavericks Dancer rehearsals she would get dizzy all the time, but what I recall most is how everybody complimented her on how good (thin) she looked. Even though at the time I was not on weight probation like Lisa, I ached for that same praise and approval. I thank God she's not dead and ask for His forgiveness for not stepping in to help. Lisa wasn't eating at all and as if that wasn't enough, she was taking the infamous diet drug Phen-Fen.

Phen-Fen was a combination diet drug that was prescribed by a doctor and was popular in the late 90's. Many of the dancers went to the same "diet Doctor" to get these pills. It was popular because you could lose a lot of weight easily and fast without exercise. Lisa could take half of a pill and not be hungry all day. Although you have to be under a doctor's care to get the pills, that doesn't mean that the doctor cares who he or she makes his or her money off of. At that time, the dancers kept the "diet doctor", as we called him, in business. Luckily, these pills were taken off the market after it was uncovered that they could cause serious health problems. Ironically, an irreversible heart condition would not be as risky as being overweight to some people. Maybe if I hadn't been so in awe and stepped up to say something to help Lisa, Kimberly and I would have had a fighting chance.

In 1996 I had been cheering for the Mavericks organization for four years. I pretty much

grew up in Dallas' Reunion Arena. The entire time I was an employee for the Mavericks, I would describe my work ethic as prompt, hardworking, dependable, respectful, loyal and obedient. I felt I was cared for, like I was family. In December of that year, I married the man of my dreams and developed strong feelings that I didn't want to spend as much time away from home. I prayed about it, and reluctantly decided that this would be my last season as a Mavericks Dancer. Although it was a difficult choice, on most days I felt good about my decision.

The hardest day came when auditions for the next year's squad rolled around. I did everything to stay busy so I wouldn't let myself think about it. I couldn't call Lisa because she was re-auditioning and I didn't know Kimberly yet. I made it through the day, but not for reasons you might expect. Later that evening, the Director called and invited me to come back and be a member of the squad. They were unable to get the talent from the audition they had hoped for. The bottom line was that they needed me. I was truly honored and I thought it was a sign from God so I said, "I'll do it". How many people can actually say that they were personally invited to be a member of a professional dance team? She only had to ask once because I was not prepared to let the Mavericks down. Here goes another year!

A few weeks after the Christmas holiday, a comment from management regarding the dancers' weight had made its way to the girls. We had *"overdone it"* on the holiday helpings. The following morning, I received a call from the Director, telling me that "the Mavericks" recommend that I *"take the week off"* to lose as much weight as I could. She also informed me that I had been cut from the next game, which was in a couple of days, that we had already rehearsed for. I wonder if they really expected for me to think I was on a vacation. She also announced that I was on a "wait and see" program, which basically meant that whenever the organization felt that I looked good (thin) enough, I would be allowed to perform on the court. I guess I was truly caught off guard because normally, when there is a problem with a dancer's weight, she is given a warning and then re-evaluated after a while. If at that time no improvement had been made, she is not allowed to perform and put on probation until further notice. Unfortunately, I was not shown this same courtesy. In my five-year history of dancing for the Mavericks, I had never seen this happen. I thought I must look like some kind of monster for them to take such drastic measures.

After I hung up with the Director, many thoughts were racing through my head. To get cut indefinitely without warning meant I must have been huge. I had never been in this situation before. I was so angry. Nobody who loves me took the time to tell me I was as big as a house. Neither my husband nor friends felt the need to even warn me that I was getting fat. Was I so big that even the people that love me couldn't bring themselves to tell me? I couldn't believe it. Nobody said anything and I felt betrayed by them all. I was ashamed and embarrassed. I had failed at something.   Before that day, I never really worried about my weight, but after that, it has consumed my every thought, and still does.

When my thoughts had finally arranged themselves, I listened to them and obeyed, but I knew then that the voice was not mine. I obeyed because that's what I've always done so well. If I mess it up, I fix it and think about who was right or wrong later. At that time, I could never have verbalized it, but now I know exactly what that voice said to me that day. *You have to have the most perfect body in the world*. So even before I hung up the phone that day I knew what I had to do. That's when the ball starting rolling in my nightmare.

Surprisingly, before that day I had only been in a real gym a handful of times and had no knowledge of where to begin. All I could think of was I had to get to a gym and fast. Recently, while teaching private dance lessons, I met a female personal trainer, Bylee Jo O'Mary. She was the first person I thought of who might be able to tell me what I needed to do. I called her immediately and explained that I needed to lose weight as fast as I could, so we met the following day. Bylee Jo, B.J. for short, asked me to wear something revealing so that she could see my body, and I obeyed (I'm really good at that). I was anxious to get started on my program and I will never forget standing in the bathroom of Brickhouse Gym, waiting for B. J. to point me in the right direction.

After a few minutes, she looked at me with honest, sad eyes and said, "There's nothing I can do for you". What!!? She continued by saying, "I can only change your shape, not make you thin." As she complimented me on my athletic figure, I went along with her program because I had no other recourse. I didn't believe her. I decided to triple everything she told me to do, and thought that would give me the results I needed, in the time I needed. She then told me what I should eat and we met at the gym everyday that week.

I seriously enjoyed working out. Brickhouse Gym had soon become my second home. I felt so comfortable there. When I completed my daily, sometimes twice-a-day workouts, I felt like I could handle whatever the world wanted to throw at me. Looking back, I no longer believe that to be true. I felt powerful because each time I went to the gym I was admired in some way by the staff or other members. People would actually ask me things like how long I had been training, or how they could make their bodies like mine? I was flattered, confused and mad. I had no idea, until B. J. told me, that people train years to build muscle that I can grow in no time. Thanks to my father, I am naturally muscular and thanks to my mother, I have a petite frame.

98

Never before had I felt so beautiful than I did in that gym.

I had not been back to a Mavericks Dancer rehearsal in a week. I spent every moment working out. I quickly became obsessed with working out whether I was at the gym lifting weights, at aerobics class, running or just in my living room with a video. About a week later, I was called and asked by the Director to report to a rehearsal to learn some new choreography. I did what was asked, but I didn't want to go. I felt like all my energy should go toward losing weight, not learning a dance routine I can't perform until who knows when. The dancers spend an amazing amount of time together. We were like sisters and I missed being around them so much. As we were practicing, I saw something that confused me even further. We rehearsed at the Coppell House of Dance, and as should be, the walls are covered with mirrors. That day I did something I have never really done before; I compared myself to every other girl in the room. I looked at myself and looked at them over and over in comparison until I felt sick. I realized that I could see my abdominal muscles, but when I looked around the room, I noticed flabby stomachs. I didn't understand...this didn't make sense...I couldn't breathe. My brain had enough and it seemed like all my emotions and thoughts started to fight with one another while I was stuck in the middle. I just couldn't handle it, so I ran. For the first time in my life, I just looked at the door and ran. All the noise was so loud and too much. I ran until I couldn't hear the noise anymore. I thought the further I ran, the softer the noise would become. If I ran far enough, maybe the noise would stop. I was running from the voices of judgment and confusion. That night, I ran out the door to the gym where I felt safe, but I didn't really stop running from those feelings, ever.

A few days after that, I did something that had been inconceivable to me before this moment, I quit the team. I thought that if I quit the team it would make all those feeling go away, but the damage was already done. I told myself I was leaving the team to protect myself from more crap, but I was already screwed. All that free time gave plenty of room for me to go crazy. My exercise routines increased in frequency and intensity and I started to monitor everything I ate. I was so anal about the food. The food I ate had to be low in carbohydrates and high in protein or I wasn't having it. At first, I would get terrible headaches and almost pass out after working out, but I became accustomed to it.

On the outside, I appeared happy and healthy, but really I was shattered and lost, trying to find the pieces to put myself back together. I believed that when I begin to feel the way I felt before this all happened, I would stop. One day, my husband, Scott, was making me lunch, and while separating the eggs and yolks he accidentally got a little yolk in the bowl. I was so angry with him. I just couldn't believe he could do such a mean thing. I was beyond the control issue, I honestly wanted to injure him in some way. In my messed up head, I actually thought he did it on purpose. Of course he didn't, but I couldn't see that. I wondered if everybody was in on it, trying not to let me see how big I was. But I saw it and I hated it. I hated what it felt like to hate myself. More than once I'm sure he was on the verge of either leaving me or having me committed, but he never did. That is what I think is so awesome in my life, unconditional love from family and friends.

When things hit close to bottom, working out was like a drug for me. Everything I did had to somehow, some way benefit my physical self. If I couldn't get that high, for whatever reason, life sucked. One day, I woke up at the crack of dawn to go to the gym to realize that, unfortunately, it had iced and snowed over and my gym was about 20 miles away. Drama... I jogged around my apartment in layers of clothes for hours. It was as if one day of not working out was going to make a big difference. It didn't matter though...all I wanted was not to be thin but to feel thin. To feel good. To feel like a woman. To be attractive. I constantly fought to get the image of me standing alone center court, at the Reunion Arena, out of my mind. The arena was full of fans, they were all whispering to each other of how I had turned into a cow. That state of mind sounds silly to me now but it is the truth.

Looking back, I realize that I learned to associate happiness with thinness. If I am experiencing a lot of stress and feel fat, I can't cope. Every situation seemed hopeless! But if I'm feeling thin, it's all good! Bring it on! There is nothing I can't handle. The world may be caving in around me, but at least I can still fit into my size 2 Gap jeans. If I find myself suffering in stress, resulting from money problems, job changes or just feeling not liked, these feelings trigger something. My brain clicks and a light bulb goes on. Duh, I think...I'm having all these problems in my life because I'm not at my ideal weight (what ideal?). The only way I could make myself feel better was to be thin, no matter what it took.

I stayed super thin by controlling everything I ate and exercising like a mad woman. Everyday I participated in some kind of exercise whether it was the same thing each day or something different. Running was good, but the Stair Master was my best friend. I could really target my hips and thighs. At the gym I went to, the Stair Master was right by the mirrors. I thought I could actually watch my butt get smaller. Some days I wished I could just live there.

.

Along with all the exercise, my diet also got worse. At first, I would eat fine through the week and splurge on the weekends, but that didn't last long. It wasn't effective enough for me and I soon stopped rewarding myself on the weekends. My husband looked forward to the weekends because we could go out to eat and it made him happy to see me eat normally. What he didn't know was that as soon as we'd get home, I would take laxatives to get rid of the food.

To this day, I am amazed how one small thing or sentence someone says can trigger another and then turn your entire life upside down. One small thing can make you suppress all that you know to be right and cancel it all out. The only reason I didn't go off the deep end is because I have such a strong family life and faith. At that time in my life, I had to re-focus my energy toward my spirituality and God. He was the only one who I would allow to help me. I also found an outlet for the negative and controlling energy I was feeling. B. J. encouraged me to take up the only sport I could enjoy competing in, fitness pageants. If you want to do well in fitness pageants, you have to eat. I have since competed in one regional pageant and received fifth place and will try to follow up with another one when this book is finished.

Of all the inadequacies in the professional cheerleading field, I feel the biggest is in this department, at least in my experiences. It seems that no real thought has gone into how serious, sensitive and potentially dangerous these standards and the enforcement of them can be. The immediate result is that you have a skinny squad. Later on you end up with emotionally confused women, eating disorders and unhealthy bodies. Is it really worth it?

If someone is going to be telling another person how they think that person's body should look, some things must be considered: They should have some sort of knowledge of what they are talking about, and possess some bit of education through school or experience. Each person's physique is unique. Some people will never be thin and healthy at the same time. What I mean is, it may be possible for them to get skinny, but only by starving themselves. For example, once I attended a Dallas Cowboys Cheerleader prep class before auditions. After the class, I approached one of the Directors and asked if I could improve in any areas. To be honest with you, I was really talking about my dancing, but she thought otherwise. She answered with, "Stop going to the gym." A.l.r.i.g.h.t.y then...this was way before I had ever been to a gym or worked out with weights. Now, if she had some small bit of knowledge, she would have said, "We would like for you to be more lean." Instead, she was asking me to lose muscle. That wasn't going to happen by simply not going to the

gym. Every women needs to be considered individually. It needs to be determined if it is possible for their body type to even look the way the organization is considering. By not doing this, you run the risk of the dancer resorting to something drastic to get the desired results too quickly.

Also, the Mavericks organization at the time does not provide any assistance once the dancer is asked to alter her body. She is expected to figure it out on her own. At least provide some outside help if they don't want to educate themselves, so that these ladies are not left hanging. I have a great idea, let's pretend we care!

It is also common practice to hire dancers on the contingency that they drop a few pounds. While I was the assistant director for the Mavericks Dancers, I witnessed this first hand when it happened to Kimberly. Kimberly and every dancer before and after her, if asked to agree to this...will. If they didn't want to be on the team, they wouldn't be at the audition. The ladies agreeing to lose weight on the spur of the moment, do so without the forethought of gym memberships, buying special food and personal trainer costs. This can run up to and over $400.00 per month ($50/food, $300/trainer, and $50/gym). I feel the organization should have provided these amenities regardless if a dancer is "out-of-shape". If looking a certain way is so imperative to them, <u>they</u> should pay, not the dancer who receives minimum compensation

It is not a responsible choice to hire a dancer on conditions of weight. You are laying the blueprint for future problems, for you and her. Ever consider that these problems can stay with them for the rest of their lives? It's just not worth the risk of being responsible for that. Dancers/cheerleaders should only be hired if they possess the figure the organization desires them to have, at the time of the audition. If from there, her body changes, only then should it be brought to her attention, not when it's already too late. There should be adequate warning. Weight doesn't normally melt away. It's a process and I don't think a lot of men involved realize this. I guess it is easier to <u>pretend</u> to grasp when you are on the other side.

I live for the day when a man who otherwise does a fabulous job, is subjected to the same unrealistic physical scale. Having said that, I do think men would not be affected so deeply and mentally. They are not pressured in the same way. Even though women come in all shapes and sizes, the average woman is not skinny! Then why, I have to ask, is it that I see thin women everywhere? Billboards, magazine covers, TV, etc. As a result, the subject of weight and body image need to be approached with great care, caution, and compassion and not in passing. If a cheerleader forgets her pon poms, she is cut from the game. Not being thin enough is not an equivalent demerit, but the consequences are similar.

Unfortunately, many years later, I still find myself standing in the mall, starring at people, wondering what it would feel like to be in that skinny body. Even while watching my favorite soap opera, I notice which actors are thin and can't help but think that I should be that way. I wish I could talk to them, not for an autograph, but to find out how they did it. It's almost like you want to surround yourself with people you think are as obsessed as you are, and they will understand when nobody else can. They can understand that your whole life revolves around your body, because you know that people judge you first on looks alone. So, what this whole drama has left me struggling with, is not wanting to believe that skinny equals happiness. Some days I don't believe it, but most days I do...because we subconsciously gravitate toward the thing we fear the most

7

TRIPLE THREAT

As I brush my teeth every morning I notice many things about the reflection. If I stare long enough into the mirror I will see the face of a black woman. Honestly, I see brown skin. The face never really changes so I don't pay much attention or think about it unless I am forced to. The subject matter of this chapter, race, may make some people, for whatever reason uncomfortable. The mention of race and how it affects us is often still difficult to talk about.

Maybe race is hard to discuss because some people are tired of hearing the same old racism subject again and again. I happen to be one of those people. Probably due to the way I was raised and the fact that I have to force myself to notice color in myself or another person. It is just not something I naturally think about. Of all the reasons I contemplated, none were compelling enough for me to close my eyes and omit this part of the book. Although I found it easier to put it away and hide, that voice inside of me reminded me that silence translates into acceptance. This acceptance is one that somehow, on some level, deep down and tucked away in a corner, I bought into. Even if you find that you feel uncomfortable, I hope that you will read on anyway. I can only

119

tell you what I experienced from the body of which I experienced it

in....a black one. I don't feel that racism has held me back, or perhaps I have just chosen not to see it, but it continues to slide its ugly way into my life and career. Of course it doesn't have to be racism in big bold letters, it is the stereotypical thinking which leads to racism; the unfairness, ignorance, bias and frustration that I discovered has left me changed.

Whenever I would begin my preparations for an audition, I definitely knew what I had to do in order to be considered for the team. Being black meant I had to be thin, pretty, and that I damn well better know how to dance. This, in a nutshell, is what I call a cheerleader/dancer "triple threat." I had to possess each of these qualities to be considered. This has always been the standard. A white woman could make the squad with one or two of the requirements, as she was measured on a different scale. Her white skin makes up for her weaker points. Once after a basketball game, my husband asked me, "Why is it that all the black girls on the team were able to dance and all the white girls could not?" I told him that it was a very good question, but I had no answer for him at the time.

Although I was lucky enough to be considered a triple threat, most of the time, it was not nearly enough. Before auditioning for a team, I had to do a little research. First, I would find out how many black girls were on the team the previous year (sometimes even in years passed) and also how many black girls would be re-auditioning. This knowledge would usually give me a good idea of my chances on making the team based on how many spots for black girls were available. If all the current black girls on the squad were returning, and the quota had already been met, my chances were slim. Unless the organization was willing to cut one "old" girl for one "new" girl. There is not a specific written rule about the number and it usually varies from team to team but it is fairly obvious that, subconsciously, minority quotas exist. I encourage you to line up the squad photos of the professional cheerleading team in your area for the past five to ten years and do the math yourself.

As expected, no one would ever be honest enough to say it, but for whatever reason there can't be too many minorities on a team. There also isn't a magic number, but if I had to guess I would say on a team of 36, between two and seven is a reasonable range. Even smaller numbers sometimes exist for Latinos and Asians. Boy, that makes you feel good to know that even if you qualify, there just may not be room for you. I can say with some confidence that if ten black girls auditioned that were thin, beautiful, and talented, not all of them would make it! It's okay to have a squad full of mostly white faces...not brown faces.

I'm not really surprised that this type of policy is practiced in professional cheerleading because I first learned how things really work in high school drill team. While cleaning out old boxes from a previous drill team director's years in charge, I came across some old score sheets. On the score sheets, next to the students name were the initials B, W, or M (which stood for Black, White or Mexican). I really didn't understand why the number of minorities was consistently low. At first, I thought they were trying to make sure the team was understandably well rounded! The real purpose of this system was to guarantee that they would have some minorities, to make it look good so that no one complained. I found it insulting that people actually think that by "allowing" a few minorities on the squad, maybe nobody will question otherwise.

This system sends the most pain filled subconscious message, and after years of hoping I was wrong, I can only take what it means one way. It takes the beauty and attractiveness of ten black girls, to equal the beauty and attractiveness of one white girl. I can't explain why the people who make these decisions believe that to the general public, women of color are perceived not as accepted or sellable as white women. For those people, and I hope it's a small number of people, I invite you to go out with a group of my black girlfriends and I guarantee you will re-think your opinion. Better yet, ask my very Caucasian husband.

Another reason for the cause for the low number of minorities is that the judges can't step out of themselves for the duration of the audition. What I mean by this is, the judges and directors tend to lean and select according to what equals them. They pick dancers that look like them! This is very necessary and natural to the person doing the choosing, but we have to recognize that this can be very unfair if done without consciousness. Speaking as a judge, I

often have to step outside of myself to ensure that the emotions I have, good or bad, do not impair the purity of my decision. Think about it! If a white girl auditions with perfectly large breasts (more so for Dallas Cowboys Cheerleaders than the Mavericks Dancers) and no talent, that's good enough to make the squad. The administration would block out and work around her short comings. In my experience, she would have a better chance of making the squad than a black girl with the same "credentials".

The favoritism was sometimes so obvious to me, but I didn't believe they (the administration) were aware...or I didn't want to believe they intentionally did it. Early in each season, a photo-shoot is scheduled to take basic group photos and/or individual head shots. These pictures are used for signing autographs and giving out to fans at appearances and games. One year, I was cheering for the Dallas Cowboys and I was really pumped up because it was head shot day. Still in disbelief that I was picked to be a member, this process made everything seem

128

real. I had made it through all the auditions and training camp, and as long as I didn't make any mistakes, me being a cheerleader was about to be official with the simple click of a camera.

There was a white (blond hair and blue eyed) girl scheduled to have her head shot taken before me. If you were next in line, you could stand near the set and watch. As she was getting ready to be photographed, I noticed that she was surrounded by the director, choreographer, make-up artist and hair stylist. They were making adjustments and ensuring that every detail looked perfect. They double-checked what her hair and make-up people had done in the other room between each picture that was taken of her. I assumed, this was to make sure that each one was flawless. This process lasted about twenty minutes or more.

While I was watching this, I found myself excited to have my chance to feel how she must have felt, important and pretty, just like a princess. I tried to contain my anxiousness as her session finally ended and mine began. After I sat down, I noticed that nothing was happening. I was not feeling very pretty at all. Why? Because the people that were in the room had left. The photographer then posed

130

me, asked for a smile, proceeded to take a few shots, then said, "Thank you." There was no pausing in between to assure perfection. No...not for me. The entire shoot was practically over before it started. I didn't think a whole lot about it at the time, but I didn't feel anything like a princess then. I could put a smile on and make myself think that there was some simple and harmless reason for this. That would be the easiest thing for me to do...but it is not the truth.

When I was a little girl, I remember I loved to spend the night with my cousin, Rachel. We would play school, put on dance recitals and change our names to something

more interesting like Bianca and Olivia. Most
often, when we played dress-up, we pretended
we were white. At a very young age, we
already had experienced the influences of the
American standard of beauty, and naturally we
innocently wanted to copy it. Along with
pretending that we were not black, we would
make it look like we had long, straight, flowing
blond hair. We would create this illusion of
beauty by placing slips on our heads. Yes,
lingerie slips. Underwear! I think this type of
child's play is normal, but what I don't get is
why we didn't want to be black women with
long, flowing, straight hair? Believe it or not,
we would somehow sneak past our parents
and go outside with slips on our heads.
Playing inside the house didn't seem real

enough. We actually rode our bikes, with confidence, through the neighborhood. We did this because we wanted to be just like the beautiful white women we watched on TV. This is not just an old phenomenon. Look on television, magazine racks or even your local sports organization's cheerleading squad... whose face do you see 80% of the time? It sure isn't a face like mine.

Since the beginning of my first year as a professional cheerleader, I have worn hair extensions, better known as a hair weave. This is an expensive process done by professionals who braid very small braids close to the scalp, then tracks of hair are sewn on to the braids. With this European invention, you can have long hair instantly. I have worn them to make my hair appear longer and thicker and my husband, who I have known for almost 20 years, has only seen me without them in photographs taken before my cheerleading days began. The reason I wear them is the same reason I rode my bike through the neighborhood with a slip on my head. I feel prettier with them in, even though my real hair is longer than it has ever been. I have grown up in age and matured, but the things I have learned since have unfortunately not convinced me that the standard of beauty is different today than it was in my childhood years.

In the Dallas Cowboys Cheerleaders, I learned that they use long hair to make black girls appear more glamorous. While in the final stages of a long audition process, right before the final tryout, each girl is evaluated individually to create her own optimum self. If you read between the lines, this means my attractiveness was being evaluated. The official hairdresser was ordered to get my hair on my shoulders, and he did through the magic of extensions.

After the audition was over, I made the squad and was repeatedly complemented by the staff at how great I looked with the extensions. I even felt like I was pretty hot!

The rest is history, but I must finally add that at least the Cowboys had the decency to pay the costs of this expensive ($3000.00/year) process. Later when I was cheering for the Dallas Mavericks, if the organization wanted a black girl to have long hair, she would have to pay for it herself. This was because the dancers in the past were sponsored by a salon, but the salon normally did not fix black hair, let alone do hair extensions.

The thing that puts the cherry on the cake of my day is that among teammates, a minority's level of talent is considered to be a result of genetics. It could not possibly be that I had worked my tail off to do a good job. All that time I spent rehearsing, studying, perfecting, and preparing was just chalked up to fact that black people naturally had rhythm. As if I hear drums in my head or something. Why is it that whenever a person of color excels at something, other people degrade that by saying it's natural and not that they worked harder than everybody else?

I believe that our problems just don't pop up overnight. They build upon each other, one on top of another, and before you know it, you have a situation. I chose to do everything I did with 100% passion because I felt like that was the only way. As a black woman, I am not expected to just do well. I only have two options: I can either fail miserably, as expected, or over achieve, because nothing in the middle counts. I can't just be regular. My black regular is not good enough or equal to white regular.

8
STEP CHILD

Along with minorities, women have had to endure their share of the struggles for equality, hoping for equal compensation, a voice and sometimes basic respect in the work place. One would think that as the professional cheerleading industry grows, and continues to play a bigger and more visual role by contributing to the overall success of sports in America, that the issues above would automatically be practiced. Let's face it, it may be rare, but some teams are so bad that the crowd actually looks forward to the team leaving the court and the cheerleaders taking their place. Unfortunately, too often these ladies are used, dismissed and overlooked without any concern or internal safety nets in place for their protection.

At the start of every Mavericks basketball season, an amazing amount of energy goes into selecting an attractive squad with dancers who possess beautiful bodies. For those who don't know, a beautiful body would imply a skinny body. As I have witnessed from the inside and out, the perfect package of a dancer is one that is physically pleasing to the eye. Whose eye? I am still trying to understand. In addition, many more hours are spent picking out just the right costumes and making sure they fit the dancer nicely. Now, try not to laugh out loud but back then, the Mavericks

Dancers are routinely accused of being too sexy or of dancing too suggestively. This judgment does not come from the public, who I would expect, but from people inside the organization. Individuals like the family and friends of people employed by the Mavericks, husbands or wives of employees, all of whom have absolutely zero to do with the dancers. During my last year as Assistant Director of the

Dancers, we actually had to pre-approve each costume with the owner's wife. WTH? This seemed like a pretty ridiculous measure especially considering that, at the time, the costumes had already been purchased. So if there was a problem, the money was not in the budget to adjust anything.

I hate to be the one to break it down for you but cheerleading is about sex, at least to the average person. You can say it's not, but believe me, it is. Men don't fantasize about cheerleaders because they look angelic. Let's try and stay in the realm of reality. If it was not about sexuality, then these ladies would be performing with no make-up on, turtle necks and floor length skirts. It has always been puzzling to me how so much time is spent scoping out the perfect (attractive) girl, and then the <u>organization</u> spends the whole season asking them not to be exactly what they chose them for.

I will never forget the feeling after a great performance as a Mavericks Dancer. I recall waiting patiently in the dressing room for the Director's comments regarding the routine, only to hear nothing about the dance. Instead, we were forbidden to wear that particular costume again because the back

was showing. The big man in charge (owner) said that, "The back is just not attractive." I felt as though I had just come back from posing nude. With every comment he made, I felt more dirty. I felt dirty because the goal was for us to not be sexy in any way, but the whole premise was based on sex. None of the girls wanted at all to be more provocative, and no one from the Dallas area could ever say that the Mavericks Dancers were too sexual. Routinely, and especially if you cheer for a then losing team, the organization often chose to obsess about silly things. When the team can't win a game, a pair of pantyhose sticking out can send the CEO into convulsions. This energy always seemed to be displaced. I remember wondering if the people in charge didn't have anything better to do.

I also mistakenly made the assumption that the Mavericks organization would be more concerned with the safety of the dancers. The Dallas Cowboys Cheerleaders' organization sets the best example in this area that is of great concern to me. With the Dallas Cowboys Cheerleaders, a dancer/cheerleader's safety and protection is always in focus and rightfully held over all else. Understandably, after these ladies work for the Cowboys, the organization then recognizes that they subsequently are put in a vulnerable state. They are potentially at risk as a direct result of having represented the Dallas Cowboys. In the society we live in, it is possible for fans or others to go over the line, positively or negatively. I'm certain that every cheerleader has received many awesome letters from fans, but also, out of a hundred letters, one or two can keep you up at night. This is scary because you don't know when the admiration stops being harmless and starts

being serious. Each cheerleader is ultimately responsible for her own well-being, but the Cowboys have chosen to take an aggressive role to ensure complete safety.

Through good preplanning and past experience, the Cowboys organization has always supplied and/or arranged for adequate protection of its cheerleaders. Remember, cheerleaders don't go to games and appearances incognito. They are made up and dressed accordingly from head to toe. From the moment they arrive, normally via their own personal vehicles, they stand out like a red dress at a funeral.

Cowboys Cheerleaders rehearse in a supervised environment, have unlisted numbers and are escorted most every place they appear. Following each game, a cheerleader is walked to her vehicle in a secured area by an employee to prevent the possibility of someone following her home. Often, police escorts are arranged and necessary to avoid any unforeseen incidents. Despite all of the unpleasant situations I had with the Cowboys organization while representing them, I at all times felt completely protected. On the other hand, while with the Mavericks, I was consistently treated as an afterthought, what my girlfriends and I called a "step child".

It is only through God's hands that something unthinkable and tragic has not happened to a Mavericks Dancer. They are not only routinely exposed to the general public, but left at their own mercy. There are no real barriers in place to stop anyone from doing anything they want to them. In my gut, I don't believe this is an intentional act. It is simply an act of pure indifference and negligence. It is hard to protect someone who you don't value on the same level as yourself. I guarantee that if the CEO's daughter was on the team, things would be very different.

When a Mavericks Dancer arrives to perform and cheer at a game, she does so in her mandatory Mavericks warm-up suit. She then parks her car just as if she was a ticket holder. Of course, she is not made to pay, but it was not uncommon for a dancer to occasionally have to convince the parking attendant that she was really a dancer to be allowed in. Once inside the parking lot, the dancer parks in the first spot she sees, whether this be close to the arena entrance or not. She then proceeds, while carrying bags that are clearly marked and holding costumes, poms, make-up, etc. She enters through the front doors and reports to the dressing room. Dancers usually report to the arena at around 5:30 p.m. and don't exit till about 10:30 p.m. A majority of these women arrive at the arena having come straight from work. After arriving, they will rehearse for one or two hours before the game starts.

As you might suspect, you could get hungry after all the sweating in pre-game rehearsal. If you do, I hope you also brought your ATM card. You didn't think that the Mavericks supplied meals, snacks or even water for the girls, did you? Silly, silly. Get a grip. Most of the dancers had learned to bring food and water, if they were able to. When dismissed from the pre-game rehearsal a Dancer is then given a time to report back from the dressing area ready to dance. After being released, more than half of the girls would quickly scatter to get to their bag to retrieve their money, cover up, and then run upstairs and stand in line like any other fan to buy food or drink. The other option was the vending machines loaded with tasty, fattening treats.

During my last year as Assistant Director, the director requested water to be available and the dancers were so excited, they treated it like it was liquid gold. However, this stopped after a couple of weeks. The Dallas Cowboys Cheerleaders receive a box lunch and unlimited beverages in their dressing room at every game. During my cheering days, the Mavericks Dancers would complain softly about this wrongness. Someone would always say in the Mavericks' defense that this was luxury belonged to the cheerleaders of winning teams. I didn't buy it then and I don't buy it now.

At the conclusion of the basketball game, the dancers exit the arena the same way they enter. More times than I care to remember, I had been both pleasantly and reluctantly escorted to my car by a drunk (happy or angry) fan, hoping for I don't know what, a date or maybe more. I don't really comprehend how I had any true responsibility regarding the outcome of the game but I would routinely have to explain a loss to upset fans. Once, a young man got in my face and verbally attacked me, blaming me in a very threatening manner for the Mavericks loss of a game. He approached me just as I was getting close to the parking area, loudly called me every name in the book, and demanded to know why we couldn't win the game. Obviously, I had no answers for him. All I could do was apologize for the loss, but he was not convinced of my sincerity. As he yelled louder and came closer to me, I wondered if he was ever going to give up. I also wondered if dealing with this was in my contract. Thank God he finally gave up and I arrived at my car safely, just a little nervous and shaken. This particular man stopped harassing me on his own, but what would have stopped him if he had other ideas? The truth is, nothing. Nothing would have stopped him from hurting me, if that's what he wanted to do. I just got lucky! I have never been hurt in the parking lot, but the potential is there and what are they waiting for? Let's do something before anything bad happens.

I am not implying that these ladies are some big time stars and need 24/7 protection. What I am saying is, since the system insists that cheerleaders go beyond the call of duty by being human billboards, or by not letting them be real people, it is only fair for the organization to give some sort of illusion of compassion. They should give back equally what they take (you should never take more than you give).

Interestingly, I have found that not only are the dancers treated with a "by the way" attitude, they are also cheated over and over in other areas. It is not out of the norm for a dancer to have to beg and plead to get compensated for work already done. Included in the Mavericks dancer's salary, she receives an amount for each game worked, in addition to two tickets to every home game. When your very excited family or friends want to come and see you perform, you had better hope that they don't want to come when the Mavericks are playing a "good" or "popular" team. You can just get that thought out of your little head. Teams like the Lakers or Magic...forget it! Those tickets are off limits to the dancers. Sometimes the dancers aren't informed of the off limits game until a day before. I'm going to assume that they took these tickets and sold them, because in Dallas, the public really comes out to see these particular games. Okay, I can put myself in their multi-million dollar shoes for a minute and understand that they would rather make money than give the tickets to the girls for free. With that in mind, shouldn't the dancers be re-compensated in some way? Anyway? I think it is only fair. Just consider this same scenario with any other job title. Your boss walks in your office and says, "When you get your paycheck, don't be surprised when 20% of it is not there. I need it to purchase opera tickets." You wouldn't and shouldn't put up with that. Amazingly, no dancer ever said a word of complaint to anyone in charge, because that is the name of the game. You are to be seen and not heard. Just sit there, look pretty and do what they say. If you accidentally say something they don't want to hear...out the door for you. You will be seen as a trouble-maker and promptly dismissed.

I am happy to say that the Mavs have since started to provide dinner for the dancers during games. There are still areas that need adjustments and let's hope with time and education things will continue to improve.

9
GAMMA PHI CAT PHITE

Often I am intrigued with how so many people can treat one another with so little respect. Whether it's a co-worker or a stranger on the street, we can sometimes act so ugly toward others. When I was in elementary school, I can remember noticing this behavior. I thought that it was just because of age and that when I got older, people would act better. I hoped time would go by faster so I could be with more "grown up" people. When I finally made it to high school, I thought people would be sweeter and cordial toward each other. I was wrong. People still treated others badly. Automatically, I assumed that surely when I went to college everything would finally fall into place. I thought that people would treat each other with dignity because that is exactly what they deserve. It didn't take me long after starting college to realize that this was never going to materialize. I had run out of milestones to hope and wait for. In that moment, I saw the staggering truth about life, that changes a child's heart to an adult one. In that instant, I understood that my parents would one day die, evil really does exist, and most importantly that sometimes people hurt others because it makes them feel better about themselves. Unbelievable as it may seem, we sometimes intentionally and subconsciously do things only because they had been done to us.

In college, I had the opportunity to experience what sorority life was all about, but I just didn't get it. At first it seemed so fun to get to hang out and party with a group of girls that you already consider friends. But in order to become a member of this "special" group of girls, you had to go through a series of tests disguised as requirements to find out how much you were willing to do to be included. Current members were in charge of carrying out the games to see the fat rise to the top.

How far will you go to prove how badly you want to belong? The wannabe's had to answer the phone a certain way, answer the door a certain way and <u>whatever</u> else they wanted you to do, no matter how degrading. You had better hope the current members liked you because they could make your life a living hell for the week or so during rush.

All this jumping through hoops madness was to be a member of a club... a club! Just like the Spanish Club, the Country Club or the Junior League! It didn't really make any sense to me. You spend huge amounts of time pretending to be someone other than who you are so you can get accepted by people and considered a member. And for what? You get a gold pin and get to say you belong to a group? I know the answer. It's because someone along the way said that is what you should do. After seven days of nonsense I had made it through rush week and was considered a member...I felt dumb, cheated and unfulfilled. I guess I was waiting for a bigger prize for the grief I had just went through. I mean, did I march and sing through the boy's dorm at 6 a.m. for this? And what exactly did that say about me? I could have gotten kicked out of school, but I was alone in my thoughts.

` The other girls were excited and couldn't wait for the next year so they could put the new wannabe's through the same silliness that they lived through. These were the same girls who thought it was stupid and unnecessary the night before when it was being done to them. I didn't feel the same. I had gone through all that jazz so that I could wear some funny letters on my chest and have instant "friends". Now I wonder, has anybody's life ever been truly lifted by joining a sorority, and really, what is the purpose of such groups? Although I didn't have the courage or words to say it back then, I am ashamed and embarrassed that I had been so easily controlled.

A year or so later when I was a Dallas Cowboys Cheerleader, I learned that sororities come in many different forms. They don't always have Greek letters, but it's the same thing. You go through a series of tests, chase your tail, kiss somebody's ass and you've accomplished something. It's the real "American" way.

Once a girl makes the squad by proving herself along the lines of beauty, talent and intelligence, that is when the real audition begins. How bad do you want to be a part of this club and how low are you willing to go to get it? In the first cheerleader meeting, it is made very clear that "You are not a Dallas Cowboys Cheerleader, you are merely just a training camp candidate, don't dare tell a soul that you are anything otherwise." Now, it is time for the

girls who went through the wringer last year to pay you back for what they had to endure...because that makes sense?

A "rookie" cheerleader is a label for a girl who is in her first year with the Cowboys. She is not considered a person and treated like a dart board and scapegoat. It's similar to how the sophomores felt about the freshman in high school, except we are talking about grown women ranging anywhere in age from 18-30 and sometimes older. These are supposedly women of high intelligence and good common sense. They are mothers, executives, nurses,

166

school teachers and students. No matter who you may be or think you are, you are stripped and labeled a "rookie".

During my special time as a rookie, I hated every day that I had to deal with such stupidity for something that matters so little to me now. Rookies were to be seen and not heard because nothing that you have to say could possibly be important. Regardless of whether or not what you want to say is beneficial to others, you are better off keeping it to yourself. Now, if you happen to forget this rule, don't worry, you will be promptly put back in your place. If you are lucky this is done privately, but more commonly it takes place in front of the entire group in the most disrespectful and degrading way possible. A good rule of thumb is to remember a rookie is always wrong and veterans are always right! You are never to correct or contradict a veteran or look at one for too long. In that organization, a veteran is to be highly respected and is considered omnipotent.

I kept thinking to myself that if I do my job and keep my mouth shut, I would avoid any trouble. Hah! Boy, was I wrong. While rehearsing, the veterans often stepped out of the line to watch and critique the rookies' performance. I always thought this was strange since veterans are always on the front row on the sidelines while in your group. Shouldn't they be rehearsing also? I always thought of this as I was on the field dancing while at the same time calling out the next steps to the veteran in front of me who didn't know the choreography. Anyway, after the four rookies in my group, including myself, danced for the veterans that night in the studio, we eagerly waited for our comments. One veteran looked at me and said she did not want to dance by me because everyone would be watching me perform and not her! I would like to think that she was kidding and that was her strange way of complimenting me. I don't think so!! She meant it...every word of it! It was often a sore spot if a rookie was considered more talented or even prettier than a veteran.

Since veterans were often left in charge of rehearsals, they would take advantage of the situation by picking on whoever they didn't like. I found 80% of the ladies to be childish, mean and hateful toward each other. Most of the girls were strangers to each other. The new girls had not done anything to upset the veterans, except to be chosen at auditions. Every girl is seen as a threat to the other's status in the organization. The environment was always thick with tension and it was not uncommon for me to cry the entire drive home. I couldn't even remember why I was doing this anyway.

I used to think that the administration was unaware of this sort of hazing, but I know they often looked away and sometimes encouraged it. If you asked them today if this happens, part of the answer would probably include that it is tradition. What is tradition anyway? I think people use this word without thinking. Is it a good tradition or a bad tradition? Does it make sense or serve a purpose? It used to be a tradition to throw eggs at a house on Halloween, but then you grow up and start using your brain! Tradition should be something that serves a purpose, like praying before supper, not an excuse to do what you want.

Luckily, I started the Dallas Cowboys Cheerleaders along with a good friend of mine who was a few years older and had just recently graduated from Texas A&M University. Having someone I trusted, gave me an outlet to vent about how strange and backwards this organization appeared from the inside, but looking so flawless on the outside. My friend was not on the team long. She quit soon after training camp. She was very intelligent and mature, and could see what I could not. Even though I didn't truly comprehend it, I'll never forgot what she said when she broke the news to me that she was turning in her poms. She said that her parents did not put her through four years of higher education so some nineteen-year-old chick on a power trip could

treat her like she was less than worthy. Now
that is a profound statement to me today.
Funny as it may seem, it is very accurate of the
situation I found myself in. Power can be a
dangerous thing when handed out flippantly. It
seems that incompetent people can somehow
obtain a world of, what seemed like, power.
Haven't you ever met some important person
and wondered how on earth they got that job?

One of the things I enjoyed about being
a Mavericks Dancer was that the directors
never encouraged such pointless behavior that
I felt was irrelevant, degrading and immature.
This behavior was unnecessary to have a
cheerleading squad of attractive, respectful,

talented, intelligent, obedient and worthy woman. To me, this was clearly not detrimental to the idea. Rather, it was a choice to lower another human being to give the illusion that you are somehow better. Don't forget, in God's eyes there is no difference between the CEO and the person that cleans the CEO's toilets.

In my heart, I do believe a veteran member of any team should be respected because of the knowledge they hold. However, they should not be worshipped. This was always apparent during my years dancing with the Mavericks. In the Director's eyes, we were all the same. Of course, due to more experience, the veteran dancers had some benefits, but more pressure was also on them because of this. They were expected to be exceptional leaders and were always accountable for their actions, right or wrong. If we all didn't perform well at rehearsal, we all helped who ever needed it. We were a real team, helping and supporting one another. We were a family because we followed the leadership of the directors. During my experience with the Cowboys Cheerleaders, I can only name two veterans out of 20 who ever acknowledged my existence with a conversation, ever. In the Mavericks, there was always a vibe of "we are all in this together". The Dallas Cowboys Cheerleaders experience was completely opposite.

175

For example, in the Cowboys Cheerleaders' locker room on game day, if someone had a hole in their hose and didn't already have a friend to help, no one would offer to help her. In fact, they would look the other way and one might chuckle. The idea is that every time one girl makes a mistake, it makes another girl look better. The atmosphere that is created from the top gives a sense of "the more she gets in trouble, the more praise I will get" or "if she gets kicked off the squad, it means less competition for the swimsuit calendar or poster the following season". On the other hand, in the Mavericks Dancer locker room in the same situation, a new pair of hose would be coming at you from all directions.

Life would be so much sweeter if we did not have to complicate the process with the little things... things that won't matter in the end. Maybe that energy we waste making ourselves feel bigger than we are should go toward something better.

10
THE BEER

I imagine you may be thinking by now that I should just shut up, get over myself and move on to deeper and more important things. You must understand that my feelings are exactly that! Leave the past where it is. Today is a new day. Life is so short and I remind myself of this every day. There is no point in living something over again that already happened. However, I believe that if you find yourself living the same scene, even after you think you have made peace with yourself, then God wants more. God doesn't just want you to forget, he wants you on a completely different level.

During this story, try not to use your common sense. That only makes it harder to understand. Try to imagine you are on a really bad soap opera. Lets call it "The Life I Thought Was Mine". You must understand that for me, choosing this career was like being cast in that old movie *The Stepford Wives*. In this strange town, the wives' personalities are stolen and replaced by clones, designed by the husbands to meet their personal needs. They are turned into robots that don't think, just do! In my soap

opera (my life) cheerleaders look like

individuals, but you're not to the organization.

They feel they can control you, they want to

limit your every action, never-mind the

appropriateness or relevance. Trust me, if all I

had to

do to stop the insanity, to remove myself from it

and forget, I would have found a way to make it

happen.

In July of 1999, I was fired by the Dallas

Mavericks after six years. Okay, not in so

many words! I was told that my position as the

assistant director was being eliminated. That

was the exact phrase the head director of the

dancers told me. As naive as I admit I am, I am not stupid. Put any label on it you wish, if it makes it any easier to take. Personally, I have learned that it pays to live life as truthfully as you can stand. So between you and me, I was fired.

My intuition is very strong and if I listen, it is almost always correct. The director of the dancers was surprised at how well I took this news, but she wasn't feeling what I had been for the past two years. When I became the assistant director, I knew that it was important to me to not contribute any more to the insanity that already existed, but to treat the dancers with the respect they deserved while giving them a worthwhile experience. If at all possible, I wanted to avoid becoming numb or selling out (even though by taking the job I had already sold out) by making a difference. I was not surprised at being fired because I consciously put the girls' well-being first. I cared about each dancer and sometimes this resulted in me butting heads with administration.

I will never find sadness in wanting the dancers to be paid adequately and on time. I will never regret insisting the organization present them in positive light, and I will never regret not allowing the dancers to be hired out as party favors. I am sure the employees of

182

the Mavericks organization felt these situations were not a big deal, but it is never a big deal when it's not you involved. So, my gut told me that I was on my way out. I was significantly more hurt because they proved to me that they really didn't care about the dancers...if I wasn't there to do it, who would?

Before this, after the birth of my daughter, I realized something I already knew. I always believed that God was in control of my life and he knows what he is doing. Unfortunately, I never gave him control as I tried to do it myself. When in the hospital after recuperating from childbirth, I asked God to take my life and lead it wherever he pleased. I had given up trying to run it and was ready to give him complete control. To me, this meant taking every experience, emotion, situation (good and bad) and dealing. My next step was to then take what I can from it, cherish it and help others with what I had learned.

Proudly, I did just that in this situation. For a change, bitterness or anger did not swell up inside of me. I didn't want to improve and try again I just wanted out so I could finally breathe. I was truly grateful for the people I had met, the precious friends I made and the

chance to get to do what I love. I am sure some people will find that hard to believe, but that shows how much having a child can elevate how important making a difference in life is. I saw that this new opportunity was a chance for me to start being a real person, not a part of a group. I was thankful it was over until...

The 1999-2000 basketball season had started and my dear friend Kimberly, who was also former Mavericks Dancer, called and invited me to a game. My knee jerk reaction was to say no because I did not want to be reminded of the wrongness that most certainly still existed. Then I thought about it, and changed my mind. For the first time in my adult life I could go to a professional sporting event and actually watch the sport for pleasure. Of course, I had performed at hundreds of games before, but the focus had always been on my performance and appearance. I thought how fun is that. I can go to a game and wear regular clothes that don't match dozens of other girls. I don't have to worry about forgetting uniforms or arriving two hours before the game starts. **Nobody** is going to care if I have on the right make-up, earrings or nail polish. They won't even know I'm there. For the first time in ten years, I was excited about the chance to be invisible, a spectator, a fan... wow. I'll get to really see what it's like to be on the other side...it kind of gave me butterflies.

The date for the game was made and it would be a foursome of friends attending: Lisa, who cheered with me for four years, Kimberly, who also was the dance captain the previous year and another friend of ours. This was more than friends getting together to go to a game. For Kimberly, Lisa and me it was a celebration of a place we had been in the past, at different times and together, looking forward to the future and its new places.

Originally, we had planned to go out for dinner and cocktails before the game, but at the last minute we decided not to. Kimberly and I thought we would just get a drink at the game. After arriving at Reunion Arena and on our way to find the seats, we had to pass through a concessions area. Instead of having to make another trip, Lisa and I purchased one beer each and proceeded to find our seats. This worked out great because the game had already begun and we didn't want to miss the dancers performing. I was having a good time being ordinary. We laughed, talked and caught up on each other's' lives while watching the very uneventful game. At one point I remember thinking the fun was in watching the game tonight, not in being a part of the game.

Like I said before, this game was a personal thing and I did not want it to be a reunion. However, I had worked there for six years and knew a good number of employees. I regularly chatted with the sound men, the security guards, concession workers and others. During this evening, nine employees noticed us, came over and said hello, but not one fan noticed us. After a few employees approached us and spoke, I noticed some similarities in the conversation. They all, in passing, mentioned they had seen me with my beer. I didn't really pay it a lot of attention at the time. In my mind, I was being an average fan, but I was so wrong. The entire time I thought I was not being observed but I found out later I was, by the entire staff.

Strangely, a good number of the administration had conveniently noticed me walking in and I had been the subject of judgment and ridicule the entire time. You see, in the arena, all the departments communicate with each other on a headset system. This allows everybody to know what is happening at all times. It is normally used to cue the dancers to an upcoming performance, or to notify security of a brawl somewhere in the audience, etc. It must have been a slow game at Reunion this night because the headsets were used to notify everyone to look at me. Some of the staff, not fans, that approached me said, "Yeah, I saw you with your beer," and another said, "I saw you walking in looking cute with your beer". I thought, what is up with this?

While I was at the game I was oblivious to the news that was traveling around the arena through the headsets. I remember thinking, am I that noticeable? I had on blue jeans and red sleeveless shirt. Apparently, when I walked in someone with a headset noticed me and announced to every person listening to take notice.

As we left the arena, still not fully understanding what had just transpired, we all became very angry with the situation and we collectively started to gripe. What did I do

wrong....really? I did not approach the dancers, I did not parade around or stand up and cheer. I didn't even have on Mavericks colors. My whole purpose was to blend in. Why was it such a big deal? I've seen former male employees attend games and enjoy alcoholic beverages. Why was I being held to a higher standard? We complained that night, then it was stored away with the many ridiculous events in my cheerleading history vault. A week later, Lisa, Kimberly and I had lunch together and I found out more about the previous incident...more than the Mavericks probably wanted me to know. Kimberly was privileged enough to be told the Mavericks' side of the story and she passed it on to me.

At the game, someone from administration asked several people if they saw

P'nut sitting in the stands drinking a beer? They couldn't believe that I would do such a horrible thing, considering that people still associated me with the dancers. They even mentioned the disappointment in Lisa, because she had a beer. Keep in mind, she has been out of cheerleading longer than I have. Okay...now I'm pissed off!! Most of all, I'm hurt! I felt like I was in tenth grade.

Let me just start with the fact that I was taught, and perfected my beer drinking techniques, with the Mavericks dancers after every game. I would also be curious to know how many fans actually even knew I was there, let alone the fact that I was drinking a beer, which, by the way, took me three quarters to finish. And when the hell did I become the poster child for the Mavericks? I honestly don't remember reading anything in any contract I signed about becoming a figure head for the Mavericks. In the <u>dancer</u> contract, there is a rule of no drinking in uniform, that's it. I would not be surprised to hear that the new dancer contract was adjusted because of me. I'm not really keen on how that applies to me or maybe I didn't get the memo.

Ironically, it was also said in praise for good behavior, "Look at Kimberly, she's not drinking a beer". Well, how stupid do they feel after knowing the only reason she wasn't was because she was hung-over from the night before?

What makes this whole thing so childish is that the Mavericks sell beer at the games. It's not like I brought it in from the car. I could even understand if I was falling over myself drunk, but I nursed that one beer for hours, three and a half quarters to be exact. What the hell? They monitor me more than the players whom they pay millions of dollars to, who overdose on drugs and get arrested.

Listen carefully...I am a twenty-eight year old mother, wife, worker, law abiding citizen and yes, former Mavericks dancer. I will do what I want, anytime I want, without regard for the Mavericks. In honor of myself, each and every time I go to a basketball game I will have three beers and wear a T-shirt that reads:

I'm a former dancer

I'm a person

And I love beer!

Of course, I would never do anything like that, but they don't realize that putting up with this twisted organization for six years entitles me to a long stiff drink!!

11
HYPOMONE`(hoop-o-mo-nay)

Writing this book has been the beginning of personal rediscovery, almost a rebirth. It is a rebirth of my determination to live my life as it was originally intended, as a child of God. I wanted...I <u>needed</u> to find out how this good little girl got so caught up when her dream turned out to be a delusion. I had to make myself see why, against everything my heart knew, I continuously chose to not see the truth. If I wasn't seeing, I wasn't living, and then I was just wasting space and that made me ashamed. I brought you into my journey not nearly soon enough because it all began years ago in a small classroom in Dallas. I want to share it with you so that you can completely grasp the lesson to the next.

Have you ever had what I call a memory tornado? That is, whenever something hurts you so deeply it triggers a switch in your brain, and then the emptiness all the times before when you felt the same pain, comes flooding back. It's like a tornado spinning your experiences out of control and scattering them to who knows where to be found who knows when. It's like watching a sad home movie of your spirit being broken over and over again, and you can't shut it off. I used to think that I was just feeling sorry for myself and I did everything in my power to make it stop. Now, I think I was wrong to do that, to suppress and not honor all those real and valid feelings. That was my intuition, that was God whispering that he was there. Feelings are the only honest mirror into yourself, and when you shut them off, it's only a matter of time before those feeling stand up and scream to be acknowledged. For me, those images held the bottom layers together that explain my personality, layers that developed and hardened many years ago and set me on my way to the course I so easily signed up for.

When the tornado of memories spins in my head, it always stops and places me back neatly in the same place.

I was a little girl sitting in my little desk in my little elementary school classroom, wanting no more than to learn, to be liked and do a good job in class. I always remember just wanting to gain my teachers' praise by doing as she asked. After all, I was just a child. My life revolved around school and my teachers, and I eagerly wanted to learn what she had to teach. I listened and observed. I learned early to do what the person in charge wanted and if you did, you would have no problems.

It was the year that the school system in Dallas decided to assess the teachers according to how their students scored on standardized tests. These tests were given over a few days. The tests usually made me very nervous, but this time I was especially nervous, because I knew my teachers wanted us to do well. I prepared for the testing, as I was told, by getting a restful night's sleep, eating a good breakfast and bringing my number two pencils sharpened and ready to go.

As I was taking the test, somewhere between wondering when the next bathroom break was going to be and trying not to fall asleep, my teacher approached my desk. I thought she was coming over to make sure I was okay or tell me that time was up and I had to put my pencil down. She didn't do either of those things, and I still can't believe what she did. From behind her back she revealed a odd sheet of paper with small holes in it. As she carefully placed the sheet over my test form and marked through the openings onto my test I watched and thought nothing. After all, she was my teacher. I thought for sure this must have been some new, faster way of scoring. As quickly as she placed the paper over mine it was drawn back out of sight. It took me only a few more seconds to realize what had just happened.

The sheet she had was a key to the test and I was told by her to change the answers that I had marked wrong to the correct answers that she had just marked. Upon comprehending what was actually going on, I must have given her a puzzling look because she casually but seriously said, "And don't tell anybody". As she walked across the room to "help" other students my eyes followed her and I watched her do this over and over until she was satisfied.

At that point many feelings flooded over me - confusion, anger, amazement and fear. Disappointment was the feeling that I couldn't express at the time and was the one that stayed with me the longest. I knew exactly what I was supposed to do if a stranger tried to take me away, but I had no idea what I was supposed to do when someone who is in charge, and paid to guide, made me do something bad. It was inconceivable to me that my teacher would mislead me in any way, and I was caught up in the confusion that followed. I continued taking my test and wondered if we were to be caught what the punishment for something like this would be. I wanted to run up to her after class was over and shake her. I wanted to shake her hard and ask her why she would do such a thing? Didn't she think of what this was doing to her students....to me? Didn't she care about us? Didn't she love us? I loved her.... I wanted to ask her if the results were so important to her why not just become a better teacher? Did she think we were not smart enough to pass it? But I didn't say anything or shake anybody. I cared about her and I didn't want to hurt her feelings, even if it was wrong and even while she was hurting me. I wondered why our feelings were not equal, but she was my teacher and I couldn't say a word. When the test was over, I went on to my other classes as if it had just been a normal day.

A few days later, I was called out of the class and told to report to the principal's office along with a few other students. "Lord have mercy", I thought. I was afraid before, but now

I was scared out of my skin. I didn't have to wonder what the principal wanted and my worst fear was coming true. I was in major trouble. I tried to pray hard enough to convince God to make him not talk to me about the test scores, but it did not work. The principal looked me in the eye and plainly and clearly asked me if the teacher gave me, or anybody else, the answers to the test? I heard my teachers' instructions from that day in my head and I answered plainly and clearly,

"No." I heard it with my own ears. While my mouth was protecting her, my brain was telling him "Yes, yes, yes she did!" Why couldn't I have just told him the truth? Why was I protecting her when I knew it was wrong? I wonder if my entire life would be different if I had only had the courage that first time.

I was disappointed and amazed at what my teacher had done, but not enough to put my feelings on the same playing field as hers. I don't know if it was because she was an adult, because I admired her or simply because she was my teacher. By telling the truth that day in the principal's office, I would have been doing the right thing even if it resulted in pain for her. I didn't realize at the time that God had created me just as he had created her. This act alone gave me unbelievable purpose and power. As the little girl I was then, I could not feel the honor and magic of the responsibility that lies in just being.

I have always believed that you will find yourself exactly were you left yourself. Each person on this planet is uniquely created with definite intent and the ones who are lucky enough to discover this do so in many different ways. Some people find it during great tragedy in life, some see it in the Grand Canyon, some people see it in their children's eyes and some people have always known it. For me, that empowering moment came years later in another classroom as I was studying the book of James at Dallas Baptist University.

There was nothing particularly amazing about that day, apart from the fact that I was healthy and breathing. I was in class listening and taking notes like a good girl when I heard the word, "hypomone'". I had never in my life heard such a beautiful sounding word! The voice in my head said "Say it again please," and my professor did just that. I loved that word even though I had no clue what it meant. I knew I should write it down so I could keep saying it, over and over later. How could a word that has no meaning to me bring me peace? As silly as that may seem, that is just what I felt, sweet and awesome enlightenment.

As the professor went on to explain the word to the class, I listened with my pen ready to write. The passage we were studying that day was James 1:2-4. I encourage you to memorize it and say it daily:

"Consider it pure joy, my brothers, whenever you face trials of many kinds, because you know that the testing of your faith develops perseverance. Perseverance must finish its work so that you may be mature and complete not lacking anything." In more common terms, steadfast perserverance. In Greek, steadfast perserverance is hypomone'.

Hypomone' translates into steadfastness. That is how you should live your life, always striving to have spiritual endurance, allowing you to be tested and re-tested, but not being moved. When this is mastered you are left completely teleios (perfect).

James was writing to a group of people who were going through horribly rough trials. His advice to them was that they should be filled with joy when faced with difficult times, because they know that God is personally molding them. In the end, they will not only survive, but will be stronger spiritually. I believe that when we are born we come to this earth with everything we need to stay connected to God, but the world drowns that out little by little. Haven't you ever had an experience where after you learn something, you feel as though you, at one time, already had that information but you just didn't recognize or couldn't communicate it? I get that feeling almost daily!

Ever since I was a young girl, I've always had the overwhelming feeling that everything is going to be okay, like someone I can't see is going to make sure that I am provided for. Sometimes, I honestly hate that feeling. Wouldn't it be easier if I just stayed sad and negative so that I would already be in pain the next time some awful thing happened to me? I can remember, about five years ago, a friend asked me why I had to always be the happy one, the one always smiling? I couldn't answer her because I really didn't know. At one point I tried to not believe in God. My older sister had given birth to a preemie who was very sick and I prayed every day that God would make him well. The baby boy died after five days and I was so angry at God, so angry that I wanted to not believe. How could I? How could I deny something that I could feel all around me? How can you run from something that is a part of you? Later on, I

started to believe that I felt this way because my mother and father always made me feel so protected and taken care of, but I don't believe that now. I know that it was God holding me in his arms and rocking me back to comfort. And now, I have a beautiful name for what I always knew. Hypomone'. I could clearly see that all the experiences I have had, painful or not, have prepared for the experience I am in right now. Hypomone'. Joy is in the journey to standing alone. Hypomone'. God was there all the time, waiting for me to see him.

In that small moment the little girl I use to be understood. My spirit and sense of being overflowed into and out of that classroom, into the hallway and out into the street. Everyday since then, I can't find a place were I am not. I fit in just where I am. Not because someone said I did, but because I recognize the strength and power in my own creation. When my heart heard that word, in that blink, I saw how awesome my destiny was. I could feel how many circumstances had to line up just right so I could be born. I could feel the pull and force of how badly God wanted me to have the chance to do what he had hoped. It was God all that time who blessed me with all my experiences, opportunities and trials. He was speaking just to me, giving me directions and pathways. I also saw how he does the same for others. There are no accidents; nothing is for nothing. God is speaking to us in everything. He is just hoping that one day we will turn the noise down and see his gifts. It makes me sad to think of how many times God tried to show me, and I just wouldn't let myself be worthy enough to trust my own heart.

The connection was spectacular! Here we are, walking around acting as if we live separate lives, never acknowledging how much we contribute to each other, the world and its problems. **Every life that you touch and that touches you is a gift and not by chance.** It's not an accident that I was not a planned birth or that I was a professional cheerleader or that you are reading this right now. Purpose! It all has purpose. Once you realize that the whole world looks different, you act differently toward it.

With all this spiritual energy and growth came a comfortable sense of power and courage! Not like control power, but a releasing power. I felt as though all the things I had wanted to do and have done just arrived in my lap. The rest was just a matter of faith enduring time.

God would never go through all the trouble to make sure I arrived and experienced what I have if he did not have a job for me to do. We all have a job to fill, and it is your individual responsibility to be quiet, listen, quit bitching and embrace it. It is the only way to peace. I know what you are thinking. This doesn't mean that I don't hurt, cry, get jealous, make mistakes or wonder "why me?" It just means that when the tears are gone and the fit is over, peace is left in my heart because faith and hope are the same thing.

You'd be happy to know that I'm really not that different from that girl in that classroom. I've climbed a few mountains and I'm a bit scarred, but I still believe that I can change the world. If not one thing is changed because of what I have written or spoken against, it will not be because I didn't stand up and shake somebody. It's funny... for ten years fear kept me from writing this book...but now I can't remember what I was so afraid of.

12
"Sizzle"

It is so amazing how quickly my life changes. As soon as I make adjustments or yield to what I think I can't change, my heart tells me no. Routinely I ask myself if my positive way of thinking is self-torture, or the only way I know how to cope with not knowing why? While it sometimes seems like bad girls do win, goodness does not always prevail and you really do have to watch your back.

It was a new millennium and I was in the midst of my transition into a somewhat "normal" lifestyle. I was surprised at how much I didn't miss being involved with professional cheerleading. This probably was a result of being blessed with a second daughter and settling into a new job. It was a time of renewal and discovery. Don't get me wrong, I had been deeply hurt by some things in my past, but being out of that environment was a breath of fresh air. Focus came more easily and I was able to gain clarity, something I haven't had a lot of. I tried, with some success to make peace with how strangely my cheerleading career had ended. I was spiritually tired but had the strength to see that God wanted me away from cheerleading. That was fine with

220

me. For about year I did not look back. It had been easy to walk away and difficult to find peace in the madness, but I had. I wore a smile because I was proud of myself,

until...by chance I discovered that I had made peace with a red, white and black polka dotted lie.

Once upon a time I had a friend. For the purpose of this story, I will call her Vera. Vera and I met while performing in a dance group together. We were alike in many ways, from our height and big smiles, to our passion for dance. We did what best friends do like go on double dates and talk on the phone all night. We also shared our secrets, dreams and biggest fears. What I thought was so neat about our friendship was that when we met, we didn't have much of anything. Neither of us was rich or had families of our own. This was well before our careers had taken off.

Fast forward about six years. I was busy performing, teaching and cheerleading. Vera was just as busy with her promising career in another area of dance. Fate stepped in and placed Vera and I in the professional cheerleading field together. She had been hired to be the head director of a local squad and she wanted me to act as her assistant director. I happily accepted her offer, and we were both overjoyed at the opportunity to work

222

together. I remember her saying that she

thought we were a perfect team because she

was the "hard-ass" and I was the

compassionate and level-headed one.

Even though we were friends, I never let

that get in the way of my responsibilities as the

assistant director. I treated her like a boss and

I assumed that she would reciprocate in

professionalism. Looking back, I recall on

occasion doing my job as well as hers without

hesitation. Aren't you generally supposed to

do what your boss asks you to do? That is just

what I did. My official job as the assistant was

to schedule appearances, notify dancers,

attend rehearsals and games and keep track of

attendance. Over the next two years I routinely found myself firing cheerleaders, teaching and choreographing routines, acting as an understudy to cheerleaders, fetching coffee, running errands for Vera's personal business, conceiving special projects without getting any credit, not being compensated for work done, as well as other things. At the time I had no problem going the extra mile, especially since I could not see what the future had in store for me. I ultimately discovered that the whole time I was working with Vera, I was being played. For those of you are not familiar with ebonics, played means being used and then screwed over.

The two years that Vera and I worked together we developed different approaches when it came to dealing with the squad. Vera's technique usually involved yelling, cussing, insulting others, and talking down to squad members. After a tantrum, it was my responsibility to pick up the pieces. I became a mediator between Vera and the dancers. In addition, I was a sounding board and buffer. Vera's goal was to do whatever it took to get the squad to do what she wanted. My goal was to do what was in the dancer's best interest. I wanted to do what no one was ever able to do for me when I was cheering. To provide a place where women could feel protected, nurtured and encouraged.

While handling appearances I discovered a problem with procedures, safety and expectations… so, I created an appearance application that was to be filled out by any person requesting an appearance by the Mavericks Dancers. The form was required before any appearance was considered, even if the request came from inside the organization. I needed to know what the event was, the location, time frame, duties, etc. The most important requirement was that it had to be submitted at least two weeks prior to the event.

After this form was agreed upon by all parties involved, I was confident that the appearance process would begin to run more smoothly. Even after all this work, the organization continued to request cheerleaders with two to five days' notice. When this occurred I tried my best to fill the request. If I called the ladies and no one was available, that was that. On more than one occasion that was not nearly enough. Even though a procedure that was agreed upon was not followed, the organization became angry with me. They then called Vera who promptly did…what she always did. Vera called each dancer and berated them. She threatened them until they changed their schedules and plans to do the appearance.

Apparently, Vera had an opinion of me that she was never filled with any conviction to reveal to me. Vera believed that I had not been doing my job. If you recall from chapter nine, I was told directly by Vera that my position was being eliminated. Instead of just saying what she felt and then justifying those accusations, she chose to lie. Why? Why do people lie? People lie to get what they want. Vera needed me to walk away from my job without any resistance or question. If Vera was telling the truth, why would she care if I made any noise about it? She needed me to just go away because she lied. I was certainly bothered by those lies but I was pissed

228

because I was fired without the chance to defend myself.

I have always been obsessed with figuring things out. My soul wants to understand the underlying reasons behind behavior, especially behavior that is so uncalled for and obviously mean spirited. It has been crucial for me to figure out and face the reasons behind Vera's deceit.

At first, the child in me wanted to believe that Vera didn't have the heart to tell her "friend" what she really thought. The bitch in me reminds me that in all the time I had known Vera, she never had a problem saying what was on her mind, ever. As painful as it was to

229

admit, I had to come to terms with the facts.

Vera had been a fraud and a fraud hates two

things: the person that can accomplish the

same goals they can without being dishonest

or manipulative, and competition. Somewhere

along the way, I went from being a friend,

business associate or person, to simply being

a threat. This was unacceptable to her and I

had to be eliminated. Vera fired me and then

lied about it because I was providing

something to the team that she could not.

Knowledge carries power, but in this

case, knowledge also carries pain. This

information was brought to me just over a year

after I was fired. I cannot describe the intense

anger, betrayal and sadness that I went through. Most of all, I felt like my hands were tied. There was nothing I could do to right this wrong or any other wrongs. All I ever wanted to do was make a difference in the industry. I didn't want to leave it the same way I discovered it. Powerless is a good way to sum up my emotional state. I had come into this industry as a child, been changed, and when I left I was still a child...a twenty-eight-year-old, woman/child. The good news is that I knew it and I finally understood what God was doing.

God knew that I would never walk away from what I was doing because I didn't want people to think I was a quitter. God knew that if somebody I loved and cared about hurt me, I would get pissed off enough to expose what I had been through to help others. God knew that if I was ever going to make a difference I would have to start from nothing...but how?

After being "eliminated", Kimberly, and I spent a great deal of time together. We talked about life, love and just about everything else. No matter how our conversations started, they always ended up on the same subject. Cheerleading! Sometimes we talked about the good stuff but mostly we talked about the things we didn't like. For a year, we verbally created the perfect professional dance/cheerleading team. We had so much fun pretending how awesome it would be if someone would just do it our way. Then, one day it finally occurred to us that we could. We could create, out of our own good and bad experiences, the perfect team

Since we couldn't go down to the bookstore and buy a manual on this process, we just made it up. We definitely were not interested in taking over a team that was already in existence. We began by researching which professional teams in our area had no cheerleaders. One organization that came to mind was The Dallas Sidekicks, which is was an indoor soccer team. We·

focused on the Sidekicks organization because the team had cheerleaders at one time and Kimberly had a working relationship with the owner of the team, Sonny Williams. Sonny Williams was also the Co-CEO of the chain of Minyards grocery stores and Kimberly, ironically, was an advertising executive for Minyard Foods. Interestingly, when Kimberly was cheering for the Dallas Mavericks she was also a senior at SMU. Minyard Foods is a corporate sponsor of the Mavericks and Sonny has floor seats at every game. Kimberly's assigned spot to sit on court during games was directly in front of Sonny. This is how they first met. We hoped this connection would work to our advantage.

Casually, in the Minyard's office, Kimberly asked Sonny if the Sidekicks were interested in having a dance team again? He responded , "Put together a proposal and we will see." So we did. We worked out every detail imaginable and it paid off. In less than five months, our virtual team became a reality. Just in case you are wondering how this feels, it's <u>awesome</u> and bigger than us. It's surreal to imagine something and then see it come to life. But the truth came last season. During the interview process of the auditions, one of the questions was, "Why did you audition for Sizzle?" One candidate opened her mouth and said, "Because I wanted to be a part of a dance team that's based on talent and ability, not if I

could sell calendars or not."

If you have a question, request or would

like to share your professional

cheerleading story, contact Leslie via email

at PomsOnFire@yahoo.com

photos are welcome. For more photos,

information and videos of Leslie and her

work visit PomsOnFire.com

**By submitting your story and/or photos you are releasing all rights
and grant permission for use in but not limited to future
publications, discussions and interviews without compensation.*

About the Author

Leslie Shaw-Hatchard sometimes known as P'nut has spent the last 20 years performing and teaching dance throughout the U. S. as well as France, Germany and Switzerland. Her dance training began at the age of 5, and has since developed into a professional career, with such credits as performing for the National Football League, National Basketball Association, National Soccer League and the Major Indoor Soccer League.

Leslie's involvement with professional sports began in 1990 when she was selected as one of 36 Dallas Cowboys Cheerleaders from a field of over 300. In 1991, Leslie began dancing for NBA's Dallas Mavericks, and she continued entertaining basketball fans as a Dallas Mavericks Dancer for the next five years, receiving recognition in 1996 as the Dallas Mavericks Dancers' Veteran of the Year and Dancer with the Most Positive Influence. In 1997, Leslie joined the dance team for the Dallas Burn, Dallas's outdoor soccer team. She most recently was the founding Director for the new NBA D-League Texas Legends Dance Team in Frisco, TX in 2010.

For eleven years Leslie was the Company Director at the Broadway Dance Center in Garland, Texas. She regularly choreographs award winning routines throughout Texas and the U. S. She often serves as a guest instructor and professional adjudicator for

Marching Auxiliaries Dance, Crowd Pleasers drill team organization, and Half-time Entertainment.

Leslie has been married for 15 years to Scott Hatchard, a Canadian Native and resides in McKinney, Texas. She teaches full time as a dance instructor at Power House of Dance and is currently the Cheer Power Director in Frisco. As if that is not enough, Leslie is also the proud mother of 11 year old daughter, Kennedy Faith and 13 year old daughter, Madison Annlye.

15770309R00128

Made in the USA
Charleston, SC
19 November 2012